The Joyful Feast

The Joyful Feast
Liturgical Elements for Reformed Worship

—YEAR C—

TIMOTHY MATTHEW SLEMMONS

CASCADE *Books* • Eugene, Oregon

THE JOYFUL FEAST
Liturgical Elements for Reformed Worship, Year C

Copyright © 2014 Timothy Matthew Slemmons. All rights reserved. Except for brief quotations in critical publications or reviews, and acknowledged use in service bulletins for public Christian worship, no part of this book may be reproduced in any manner without prior written permission from the publisher. Write: Permissions. Wipf and Stock Publishers, 199 W. 8th Ave., Suite 3, Eugene, OR 97401.

Cascade Books
An Imprint of Wipf and Stock Publishers
199 W. 8th Ave., Suite 3
Eugene, OR 97401

www.wipfandstock.com

ISBN 13: 978-1-62032-002-0

Cataloguing-in-Publication Data

Slemmons, Timothy Matthew.

   The joyful feast : liturgical elements for reformed worship, year c / Timothy Matthew Slemmons.

   xxvi + 250 pp. ; 23 cm. Includes bibliographical references and index(es).

   ISBN 13: 978-1-62032-002-0

   1. Common lectionary (1992)—Handbooks, manuals, etc. 2. Lectionaries—Handbooks, manuals, etc. 3. Reformed Church—Liturgy—Handbooks, manuals, etc. I. Title.

BX9427 .S57 2014

New Revised Standard Version Bible, copyright 1989, Division of Christian Education of the National Council of the Churches of Christ in the United States of America. Used by permission. All rights reserved.

*Dedicated to the glory of the Triune God
and in honor of the Christian ministry and witness of*

—the Rev. C. Michael Kuner—

mentor, colleague, brother, and friend.

Then turning toward the woman, [Jesus] said to Simon, "Do you see this woman? I entered your house; you gave me no water for my feet, but she has bathed my feet with her tears and dried them with her hair. You gave me no kiss, but from the time I came in she has not stopped kissing my feet. You did not anoint my head with oil, but she has anointed my feet with ointment. Therefore, I tell you, her sins, which were many, have been forgiven; hence she has shown great love. But the one to whom little is forgiven, loves little." Then he said to her, "Your sins are forgiven." But those who were at the table with him began to say among themselves, "Who is this who even forgives sins?" And he said to the woman, "Your faith has saved you; go in peace."

—Luke 7:44–50 (Proper 6/11th Ordinary)

"Be dressed for action and have your lamps lit; be like those who are waiting for their master to return from the wedding banquet, so that they may open the door for him as soon as he comes and knocks."

—Luke 12:35–36 (Proper 14/19th Ordinary)

When he noticed how the guests chose the places of honor, he told them a parable. "When you are invited by someone to a wedding banquet, do not sit down at the place of honor, in case someone more distinguished than you has been invited by your host; and the host who invited both of you may come and say to you, 'Give this person your place,' and then in disgrace you would start to take the lowest place. But when you are invited, go and sit down at the lowest place, so that when your host comes, he may say to you, 'Friend, move up higher'; then you will be honored in the presence of all who sit at the table with you. For all who exalt themselves will be humbled, and those who humble themselves will be exalted."

He said also to the one who had invited him, "When you give a luncheon or a dinner, do not invite your friends or your brothers or your relatives or rich neighbors, in case they may invite you in return, and you would be repaid. But when you give a banquet, invite the poor, the crippled, the lame, and the blind. And you will be blessed, because they cannot repay you, for you will be repaid at the resurrection of the righteous."

—Luke 14:7–14 (Proper 17/22nd Ordinary)

Then [Jesus] said to them, "Oh, how foolish you are, and how slow of heart to believe all that the prophets have declared! Was it not necessary that the Messiah should suffer these things and then enter into his glory?" Then beginning with Moses and all the prophets, he interpreted to them the things about himself in all the scriptures.... When he was at the table with them, he took bread, blessed and broke it, and gave it to them. Then their eyes were opened, and they recognized him; and he vanished from their sight. They said to each other, "Were not our hearts burning within us while he was talking to us on the road, while he was opening the scriptures to us?" That same hour they got up and returned to Jerusalem.

—Luke 24:25–27, 30–33a (Easter Evening [ABC])

Contents

Series Foreword | *xi*
Preface | *xix*
Acknowledgments | *xxiii*

Part I: The Christmas Cycle: *Advent—Christmas—Epiphany*

First Sunday of Advent | 3
Second Sunday of Advent | 6
Third Sunday of Advent | 9
Fourth Sunday of Advent | 12
Christmas, First Proper [ABC] (*Christmas Eve*) | 15
Christmas, Second Proper [ABC] (*Christmas Morning*) | 18
Christmas, Third Proper [ABC] (*Christmas Day*) | 21
First Sunday after Christmas | 24
Second Sunday after Christmas [ABC] | 27
Epiphany [ABC] | 30
First Sunday after Epiphany—Ordinary Time 1 (*Baptism of the Lord*) | 33
Second Sunday after Epiphany—Ordinary Time 2 | 36
Third Sunday after Epiphany—Ordinary Time 3 | 39
Fourth Sunday after Epiphany—Ordinary Time 4 | 42
Fifth Sunday after Epiphany—Ordinary Time 5 | 45
Sixth Sunday after Epiphany / Proper 1—Ordinary Time 6 | 48
Seventh Sunday after Epiphany / Proper 2—Ordinary Time 7 | 51
Eighth Sunday after Epiphany / Proper 3—Ordinary Time 8 | 54
Last Sunday after Epiphany (*Transfiguration Sunday*) | 57

Part II: The Paschal Cycle: *Lent—Easter—Pentecost*

Ash Wednesday [ABC] | 63
First Sunday in Lent | 67
Second Sunday in Lent | 70
Third Sunday in Lent | 73
Fourth Sunday in Lent | 76
Fifth Sunday in Lent | 79
Sixth Sunday in Lent (*Palm Sunday*) | 82
Sixth Sunday in Lent (*Passion Sunday*) | 85
Monday of Holy Week [ABC] | 89
Tuesday of Holy Week [ABC] | 92
Wednesday of Holy Week [ABC] | 95
Maundy Thursday [ABC] | 98
Good Friday [ABC] | 101
Easter (*The Resurrection of the Lord*) | 105
Easter Evening [ABC] | 109
Second Sunday of Easter | 112
Third Sunday of Easter | 115
Fourth Sunday of Easter | 119
Fifth Sunday of Easter | 122
Sixth Sunday of Easter | 125
Ascension of the Lord [ABC] | 128
Seventh Sunday of Easter | 131
Pentecost | 135

Part III: Ordinary Time (Propers 4–29): *Trinity—All Saints'—Christ the King*

Trinity Sunday | 141
Proper 4—Ordinary Time 9 / May 29–June 4 (*if after Trinity*) | 144
Proper 5—Ordinary Time 10 / June 5–11 (*if after Trinity*) | 148
Proper 6—Ordinary Time 11 / June 12–18 (*if after Trinity*) | 151
Proper 7—Ordinary Time 12 / June 19–25 (*if after Trinity*) | 154
Proper 8—Ordinary Time 13 / June 26–July 2 | 157
Proper 9—Ordinary Time 14 / July 3–9 | 160

Proper 10—Ordinary Time 15 / July 10–16 | 164
Proper 11—Ordinary Time 16 / July 17–23 | 167
Proper 12—Ordinary Time 17 / July 24–30 | 170
Proper 13—Ordinary Time 18 / July 31–August 6 | 173
Proper 14—Ordinary Time 19 / August 7–13 | 177
Proper 15—Ordinary Time 20 / August 14–20 | 180
Proper 16—Ordinary Time 21 / August 21–27 | 183
Proper 17—Ordinary Time 22 / August 28–September 3 | 186
Proper 18—Ordinary Time 23 / September 4–10 | 189
Proper 19—Ordinary Time 24 / September 11–17 | 192
Proper 20—Ordinary Time 25 / September 18–24 | 195
Proper 21—Ordinary Time 26 / September 25–October 1 | 199
Proper 22—Ordinary Time 27 / October 2–8 | 203
Proper 23—Ordinary Time 28 / October 9–15 | 206
Proper 24—Ordinary Time 29 / October 16–22 | 209
Proper 25—Ordinary Time 30 / October 23–29 | 212
Proper 26—Ordinary Time 31 / October 30–November 5 | 215
All Saints' Day / November 1 (or *First Sunday in November*) | 219
Proper 27—Ordinary Time 32 / November 6–12 | 223
Proper 28—Ordinary Time 33 / November 13–19 | 227
Proper 29—Ordinary Time 34 / November 20–26
(*Christ the King* or *Reign of Christ*) | 232

Index of Scripture Readings | 237

Series Foreword

THIS SERIES OF *LITURGICAL ELEMENTS FOR REFORMED WORSHIP* HAS developed over the course of more than fifteen years of ministry in Presbyterian contexts, primarily pastoral but also academic. Although this development has coincided with my own vocational (theological, homiletical, liturgical, and pastoral) formation and will therefore reflect a number of vocal variations (so to speak) that correspond to different stages of this formation, the primary concern that gave rise to this project in the first place has not diminished in the least, but has taken on an even deeper and more persistent sense of gravity and conviction. What began as a practical search for a greater variety of prayers of confession and assurances than I found in the *Book of Common Worship* (1993)— and more specifically, for prayers that reflected more directly how the Church should confess in response to specific texts found in the *Revised Common Lectionary* (1992) from week to week—has become an overriding concern that informs both my work in advocating an expansion of the lectionary, as well as my labors in the area of Reformed homiletics and worship, namely, that ongoing and continual repentance from sin in all its forms is essential, not accidental, to the Christian life, to the Reformed tradition of worship, and to the vitality and viability of the Church.

Reared as so many other pastors and seminary students have been on the textbooks of the late liturgical scholar James F. White, an ecumenically minded Methodist who served on the faculty at Notre Dame, I too quickly and uncritically adopted White's dim characterization of Reformed worship that he repeatedly describes (at least in the hands of the Swiss Reformers and their Calvinist and Puritan descendants) as "heavily penitential." This negative caricature is reinforced so often by White[1] and in

---

1. James F. White, *Introduction to Christian Worship*, 3rd ed. (Nashville: Abingdon, 2000) 124, 160, 161, 189, 254, 256, et al., and *A Brief History of Christian Worship* (Nashville: Abingdon, 1993) 76, 105, et al.

the literature developed in his wake that his more positive assessment of the joy with which the same tradition sang the Psalms seems jarringly inconsistent, that is, as though the connection between repentance and the joyful freedom to be discovered therein is entirely incongruous. Equally symptomatic of White's failure to appreciate the Reformed tradition is his suggestion that Calvin simply followed the Fourth Lateran Council in requiring confession before communion, as though the premier theologian of the sixteenth century applied the scriptural regulative principle to every question but this one.

White was not alone in his superficial (i.e., dour) understanding of the Reformed tradition, of course, but his conviction that "the study of Christian worship is the best way to learn ecumenism" has been influential and probably explains why many Reformed liturgical scholars today seem more eager to shun whatever may be described as "heavily penitential" than to lay claim to the true character of the Reformed tradition as *essentially* penitential, and not merely in a manner that belongs to the medieval period, from which, the ecumenist White suggests, the Reformers were not sufficiently critical to separate themselves. On the contrary, the point that should appear obvious to those who apply the principle of canonical comprehensiveness[2] in their study of Scripture and the regulative principle to their study of the Reformation is that the Reformers, in their own exegetical labors, discerned the summons to repentance resounding throughout the canon and (despite important differences in grammatical moods) on both sides of the crucifixion, resurrection, and ascension of Jesus, and they felt sufficiently convinced and convicted by it that they sought to give it a central and essential, not an auxiliary role, in their liturgical reforms. As I have said elsewhere, this essential role of repentance is signaled at least symbolically, and perhaps definitively, in the fact that the first of Luther's ninety-five theses (1517), the initial downbeat of the Reformation itself, declares that the Christian life is one of ongoing repentance. Meanwhile, the liturgical renewal movement, driven in part by the desire to avoid medieval stereotypes, has succeeded in depriving the Reformed worship tradition of one of its greatest, most distinctive, and powerful gifts: the disciplines of self-examination and robust confession that are the hallmark of true repentance and deep "reform." The services of preparation and self-examination (that last appeared in the

---

2. See Timothy Matthew Slemmons, *Year D: A Quadrennial Supplement to the Revised Common Lectionary* (Eugene, OR: Cascade, 2012).

1946 edition of the *Book of Common Worship*) have given way before the drive toward more frequent communion, and one can only wonder at what point, if ever, the trend toward less preparation and more "celebration" will bring to mind the long forgotten and much abused dialectic of the holy and the common.

It is from this point of deep conviction that this series of liturgical resources is sent forth, not because every element will necessarily do justice to the sense in which perpetual repentance is the most frequently overlooked and distinctive "essential tenet" of the Reformed tradition (and because the most distinctive, therefore the most essential, so to speak), but for the simple fact that repentance, self-examination, confession, and the good news of forgiveness deserve far better than to be reduced to the formulaic. It may well be that those who worship in the Reformed tradition, at least those who are unembarrassed by the essentially penitential—and undeniably joyful—character of the tradition, are best positioned to lay claim to that truth and offer it to the broader Church. On the other hand, anyone who would persist in such embarrassment, I would suggest, is not paying sufficient attention—to Scripture, to the state of the Church, to the state of the world, or the state of their own souls.

This is not to say that these elements come from on high, by any stretch, except insofar as they are a response to, and sometimes a direct voicing of, Scripture. Rather, these prayers come from the pen of one who needs to pray them. They were in no instance designed to be prescriptive, but are the best response this pastor has been able to muster as one who finds himself staring down the business end of the sword of the Word (Eph 6:17; Heb 4:12; Rev 2:12; 19:15, 21). But what a startling thing it was the first time I heard a congregation praying in unison a Prayer of Confession I had written and printed in the bulletin! Having shifted my focus entirely from the task of getting the bulletin together on Thursday afternoon to entering into worship itself on Sunday morning, I was halfway through the prayer myself before I realized: "These words sound familiar." Then it dawned on me: "Oh, yes. I wrote them."

There was nothing especially gratifying about this experience, for I have never harbored any great aspiration to put words in other people's mouths. But from that moment the prospect of writing prayers that the people of God themselves would speak in worship became a particularly sobering and serious responsibility. For, in fact, there is an inescapable sense in which "finding words for worship"[3] does in effect put words in the mouths of those in attendance: individuals of innumerable dispositions, including some who may well resist assenting (saying "Amen") to them, and churches (local, denominational, and global) whose spiritual and moral conditions need to be truthfully and honestly confessed in the presence of "God and everybody." It is no exaggeration whatsoever, but theologically and anthropologically accurate, to say that the Prayer of Confession can, by its very nature as an expression and an act of repentance, "make one's flesh crawl," for repentance is a gift from God (Acts 5:31; 11:18), but "the mind that is set on the flesh is hostile to God; it does not submit to God's law—indeed it cannot . . ." (Rom 8:6–7). Prayers of Confession then must walk a fine line, balancing "brutal" honesty with tender mercy; they must break the horse, not make it bolt.

The responsibility for liturgy is incalculably heightened when one considers that such prompting of the people is no mere stage direction; yet, per Kierkegaard's *contra*-theatrical analogy, the minister or preacher *is* a prompter whose labor is done with the expectation that the people will in fact direct the prompted words *to* God. And as if *this* were not enough, the pastor and liturgist must remember that the liturgy at points entails speaking *for* God to the people—as in the Declaration of Forgiveness, which bears the liberating function of Gospel every bit as much as does the preaching of the Word. *God* calls the people to worship. *The risen Jesus Christ* heralds the good news of forgiveness. Worship is less a work of the people (who are but the minor partners in the conversation) and more a work of *the Holy Spirit*. Yet *the Holy Trinity* condescends to enlist human agents in doing all of this work (externally speaking), much of it through the pastor as liturgist. Sobering thoughts indeed.

But such a responsibility cannot be fulfilled by a formulaic approach. The routinization of worship is deadly, even if it results from the most faithful allegiance to orthodoxy. As one pastoral colleague put the problem when I entered into this project some fifteen years ago, "So how many ways can you say, 'You are forgiven!'?" That is certainly one way of posing the question. How should one answer? To begin with: more than three.[4] On the one hand, the words of Scripture themselves are the sole written authority and norm for all elements of worship, including the Declaration

---

3. See Ruth Duck, *Finding Words for Worship: A Guide for Leaders* (Louisville: Westminster John Knox, 1995).

4. *Book of Common Worship* (Louisville: Westminster John Knox, 1993) 56–57.

of Forgiveness. On the other hand, the same Spirit who speaks through the Scriptures resists distillation of the singular gospel to a single formula, but inspires ongoing interpretation, reiteration, amplification, and elaboration as required by a wide variety of human conditions; for sin, depravity, guilt, pride, and all manner of things that exalt themselves in opposition to the Word (2 Cor 10:4) may succeed against incantation, but they will not succeed against the Church at worship recapitulating the *missio Dei* in fresh, biblically faithful ways. The Word of the Lord will not return empty (Isa 55), and the gates of hell will not prevail against the Church (Matt 16) *at worship*. As J.-J. von Allmen observed (specifically with reference to 1 Cor 11–14), the term *ecclesia* first and foremost applies to the liturgical assembly; it is not primarily a sociological term.[5] This insight, clear as it is in Scripture, has yet to sink in to the mind of the mainline churches, which seem entirely bent on sociological reform. But if von Allmen was right, and I think he was, then I would contend that the diversity of the Church need not be forced to satisfy our sociological presuppositions, whether liberal or conservative, but allowed to arise in and emerge from worship itself as the Church encounters the risen Christ and the Holy Spirit speaking through the Scriptures.

Further, if we follow this understanding of an essentially liturgical ecclesiology, and an essentially repentant orientation to the Christian life, through to their logical conclusion and point of convergence, we must finally recognize the fact that, in the temporal sphere (and whether we like it or not), Christian worship cannot be fully grasped apart from the theater of spiritual warfare by which it is surrounded and from which it is protected and held *in God* as a sanctuary—a holy "safe" zone, so to speak—an assembly around font, pulpit, and table, with the whole creation (Rom 8:19), even a host of impotent enemies (Ps 23:5), looking on.

"Safe," of course, is a relative term and begs definition in relation to its distinct referents. I would not be so naïve in this day and age to suggest that physical harm cannot come to God's people in worship, but I shall say with the psalmist, "I trust in God; I am not afraid; what can flesh do to me?" (Ps 56:4) Neither would I suggest that the holy presence of God is unambiguously "safe," so as to lose sight of the "fear of the Lord" that is due him (Ps 90:11). Nevertheless, when worship is framed in this way, the Church stands to gain a much clearer sense of what is at stake, and to

---

5. J.-J. von Allmen, *Worship: Its Theology and Practice* (New York: Oxford University Press, 1965) 43.

see people of every spiritual condition avail themselves of the healing and salvific presence of the LORD, even as worship itself serves (esthetically) as creation's libretto in the theatre of God's glory, the theatre in which "the battle is the LORD's" and the Church's vocation is to remember and give thanks for victories past and promised. As von Allmen held:

> in its liturgy the Church acts on behalf of the world, which is totally incapable of adoring and glorifying the true God, and . . . the Church [at worship] represents the world before God and protects it.[6]

In other words, the Church, as a royal priesthood in Christ, has an intercessory role to play whereby its worship, as it were, actually "protects" the world. That alone should be both good news to the whole Church and good news to the world! Hence, liturgy is really not "common worship" in any sense. On the contrary, liturgy is the divine and priestly service of the body of Christ, the service of worship performed by the Church—as it is empowered, guided, and inspired by the Holy Spirit—for God and in response to God's gracious self-revelation in the Servant Lord Jesus Christ. True liturgy unfolds under the headship, under the most excellent ministry (liturgy), and in the name of Jesus Christ, the Son of God, in whom all believers together are to serve in a united yet diversely gifted priesthood, to the eternal glory of God—and (temporarily) on behalf of a liturgically incompetent and often hostile world.

These convictions, as mentioned above, have come very slowly.[7] While I hope in future to be able to articulate these concerns and convictions more clearly and thoroughly (and defend them, if necessary), for now I must admit the evidence of this unlovely developmental plodding may be all too obvious in the liturgical elements provided here and in the three companion volumes that are planned. For this project has developed contemporaneously with my own continuing theological education and vocation, and in the weekly attempt to prepare faithful worship amidst the numerous competing demands of life and ministry; thus, all stages of this development will be represented here. This will account for the varying degrees of tone: from solemnity to exuberance, from the poetic to the prosaic, from an initial concern for avoiding overuse of masculine

---

6. Ibid., 16.

7. As I say frequently and with no irony intended, I loosely translate the Latin on my own PhD (*philosophiae doctor*) degree to read, "slow learner."

metaphors for God to a more intentional use of the biblical names of God, including Lord and Lord, etc., and a desire to avoid the far greater sin of effectively depersonalizing God by the avoidance of personal pronouns. (Where the use of Lord is concerned, my intention has been to retain this reference to the tetragrammaton, YHWH, as it is rendered in most translations of the Old Testament, and thereby direct the reader's attention to the holy name as it is used in the texts that inspired the element in question; likewise, the use of Lord is meant to reflect usage in the New Testament, which most often occurs in reference to Jesus.) In light of this peculiarly developmental quality, then, the reader may find it more helpful to approach these volumes as more of an indicative historical record, as useful artifacts, than as prescriptive in any heavy-handed or "heavily penitential" sense. They are perhaps a tidy presentation of the otherwise untidy relics of many services, a peek into one pastor's file drawers stuffed with bulletins and prayers prepared for congregations perhaps very different from the reader's own. Many, if not most, of these elements, if they are to be of service to the ongoing life of the Church at worship, will invite adaptation, in which case I simply ask that those who thus adapt them will acknowledge doing so, yet remember with kindness and favor the congregations, both the saints and their pastor, whence and among whom—by the grace of the Word and the Spirit—they first arose.

Timothy Matthew Slemmons
University of Dubuque Theological Seminary
The Feast of Epiphany, A.D. 2012

Preface

THE TITLE ASSIGNED TO THE THIRD VOLUME IN THIS SERIES OF *LITURGICAL Elements for Refomed Worship* (*LERW*) is potentially misleading for several reasons. First, unique among the four volumes in the series, its origins are liturgical, deriving from the Invitation to the Sacrament of the Lord's Supper, rather than directly from Scripture.

> Friends, this is the joyful feast of the people of God!
> They will come from east and west,
> and from north and south
> and sit at table in the kingdom of God.[8]

Second, as I noted in the final sermon in *Groans of the Spirit*, the latter part of this invitation (Luke 13:29) is not included in the three-year cycle of the *Revised Common Lectionary* (*RCL*). Moreover, its liturgical use as an invitation to the sacrament wrenches it out of its literary context, since Jesus' prophecy of the great banquet comes as a direct warning to certain of his listeners that they will not be included but rather excluded from the great gathering (Luke 13:25–29).[9] Not surprisingly, this "exclusive" Lukan saying of Jesus has no place in the *RCL*.

Third, this liturgical allusion to "the joyful feast" risks the mistaken impression that the present resource offers elements to be used specifically on sacramental occasions. While nothing should prohibit the use of these elements on such occasions, a quick glance at the contents of this volume and its companions will soon correct, and perhaps disappoint, such expectations of finding prayers specifically designed for use at the Supper. Further, it may be argued that the eucharistic emphasis

---

8. Presbyterian Church (U.S.A.), *Book of Common Worship* (Louisville: Westminster John Knox, 1993) 68.

9. Timothy Matthew Slemmons, *Groans of the Spirit: Homiletical Dialectics in an Age of Confusion* (Eugene, OR: Pickwick, 2010) 117–22.

of the extant three-year lectionary is sufficiently strong that it needs no augmentation here.[10] As mentioned in the Series Foreword, it was not a lack of sacramental "Great Prayers of Thanksgiving" that inspired this series, but a relative dearth of penitential elements in a service book that represents the Reformed tradition, which, I have repeatedly argued, is essentially penitential.

Perhaps most misleading in this choice of an apparently eucharistic title is the fact that the paradigmatic "joyful feast" in the Gospel of Luke, namely, the journey to and the meal at Emmaus—a narrative that shapes our entire understanding of worship in the Reformed tradition[11]—is not specifically assigned to Year C. While it is appropriately and uniformly assigned to Easter Evening, regardless of the year, its specific assignment for the Service of the Lord's Day (presumably at the morning service) occurs on the Third Sunday of Easter in Year A, with the subsequent resurrection appearance of Jesus in Jerusalem assigned specifically to the same Sunday of Year B (Luke 24:36b–48) and generally (ABC) to Ascension (24:44–53).

Despite all these caveats, the widely noted leitmotif according to which Luke's Gospel unfolds in a series of meal scenes nevertheless constitutes sufficient ground on which to gather these elements for the third year of the lectionary when the Third Gospel is in view. Exegetically, this motif has been expertly treated by David Moessner in his classic work, *The Lord of the Banquet*,[12] while the preacher will find Kenneth L. Mauldin's sermon collection, *Table Talk with Jesus*,[13] a fine example of a scholarly homiletical treatment of the same. While it may not mitigate some readers' dashed hopes for more explicitly eucharistic prayers, it may yet help to place in a fresh light those Sundays when the Service of the Word predominates to recognize the strange fact that, in the Emmaus narrative, we have no hard textual evidence that anyone even ate anything on that occasion. The emphasis is so thoroughly on the messianic teaching that caused the disciples' hearts to burn within them, the revelation

---

10. Timothy Matthew Slemmons, *Year D: A Quadrennial Supplement to the Revised Common Lectionary* (Eugene, OR: Cascade, 2012) 26–30.

11. Hughes Oliphant Old, *Worship: Reformed according to Scripture* (Louisville: Westminster John Knox, 2002).

12. David P. Moessner, *Lord of the Banquet: The Literary and Theological Significance of the Lukan Travel Narrative* (Minneapolis: Fortress, 1989).

13. Kenneth L. Mauldin, *Table Talk with Jesus* (Nashville: Abingdon, 1979).

of the real presence of Christ at the table, and the subsequent joy of the disciples at these discoveries, that any mention of whether or not they paused to consume the elements is incidental and, supposing they did so, might even be construed as inconsistent with their evident exuberance and their rush to return to Jerusalem.

Perhaps all of this is simply to reiterate the claim of the sermon mentioned above: "The Reformed tradition is nothing . . . if it is not first and foremost a fellowship in Christ of the joyfully repentant."[14] Such a fellowship itself is feast enough for the time being; it is sustenance sufficient to strengthen us for our journey to the heavenly banquet.

§

Lastly, it may legitimately be asked to what extent a lectionary-based liturgical resource such as this belongs to the Reformed tradition at all, since historically the Reformed tradition in its most undiluted incarnations has been characterized by a preference for *lectio continua*, rather than *lectio selecta* and the observance of the church year. I make no secret of the fact that, despite my labors in the area of lectionary-based liturgy and in advocating for lectionary expansion, I recommend to students of preaching and worship that, after a cycle or two through the lectionary, they develop their skills in preaching *lectio continua*, at which point such resources as this one will become more intermittently applicable (i.e., as texts arise in series, rather than calendrically). Nevertheless, as a practical theologian, it seems to me important to offer to the historically situated church (1) what one is able, and (2) what one might reasonably hope to be received for the improvement of its present diminished and even acrimonious condition. It is the health of the mainline churches broadly, the Reformed churches more narrowly, and the PC(USA) most directly that concern me and that I hope and pray this resource will help to promote. As the *LERW* series is, like *Year D* itself, offered in a supplementary capacity, I am under no illusions that it represents some sort of liturgical ideal or definitive standard for Reformed worship. On the contrary, I will be the first to admit that its success in serving its stated ends will hinge almost entirely on matters quite beyond its purview—theological, as well as ecclesial—and, in the latter case, will almost certainly entail a number

14. Slemmons, *Groans of the Spirit*, 122.

of acute and long-overdue course corrections. With that said, may this resource and its companions serve the practical purpose of ensuring that the church's public worship and witness is scripturally faithful, as well as morally credible and theologically compelling.

Acknowledgments

ANY VOLUME OF LITURGICAL ELEMENTS FOR CHRISTIAN WORSHIP IN THE Reformed tradition must necessarily begin and end and be permeated throughout with thanksgiving and praise to the triune God. *Soli Deo Gloria!* But while the Trinity has also determined, by virtue of the grace of God's revelation, incarnation, mission, and covenantal nature, to involve and enlist many saints in the ongoing ministry of the Word and the Spirit, and while there are innumerable agents of God's grace for whom I do give thanks at this juncture, I will confine myself to mentioning those whose roles loom largest in my admittedly porous memory.

First of all, and most instrumentally, I give thanks for the two congregations I have been blessed to serve as pastor and interim pastor, respectively, for it is these congregations that first gave voice and lent their communal "Amen" to these various elements, or something close to them: Central Presbyterian Church, Tarentum, Pennsylvania (1995–2000) and First Presbyterian Church, Titusville, New Jersey (2004–2008). In the case of Year D, it was the latter congregation that served as its testing ground, and the fruits of it have been apparent.

The gracious pedagogical comments of the late Dr. Lucy Rose of Columbia Seminary continue to be instructive each time I teach worship. The prayers of the Reverend Roy Henderson at Lansdowne Parish Church, Glasgow, UK, a fine wordsmith, fed me for a year's worth of Sundays abroad, while the leaders of the Late Late Service, also in Glasgow, challenged me by example to think through the words used in worship with painstaking care (1992–93). Dr. Fred Anderson's labors at Madison Avenue Presbyterian Church and his enormous contribution to the worship of the Presbyterian Church (USA) are well documented, and I am grateful for the encouragement he has offered in our few, brief, but memorable exchanges.

The shape of Lavon Bayler's resources, *Taught By Love*, *Led By Love*, and *Gathered By Love* (United Church Press), which I ran across in 1996 and have used on occasion, inspired the notion that I might be able to build a similar resource over time, but in a more Reformed voice and vein.

Dr. Richard Young, now at Orchard Park Presbyterian Church in the Buffalo, New York area, offered encouragement early on, and was a rare and delightful conversation partner as we were both serving in western PA.

My professors at Princeton Seminary, specifically, Dr. James F. Kay (now Dean), Dr. Sally Brown, and visiting lecturer Dr. Hughes Oliphant Old (now Dean of Erskine Seminary's Institute for Reformed Worship) prompted more critical (and self-critical) thinking about liturgical concerns, and I am grateful for their instruction in seminars, in their pedagogy, and in their scholarship.

I am also grateful to the First Presbyterian Church, Topeka, Kansas, which has served as my "safe home" sanctuary for going on fifty years. I am especially grateful to the long line of ministers, musicians, and other saints who have served that congregation over the years, and maintained a highly esthetic doxology; the Reverend C. Michael Kuner, who once served the church as both Associate Pastor and later as Interim Head of Staff, is my brother-in-law and has served as a mentor for many years; Mike's wife and my sister, Jennifer Kuner, has often filled the sanctuary with her exquisite solo (and choral) contributions, carrying on the contralto reverberations our mother first put in motion there beginning in the 1940s. My brother Rob and his wife Julie have always been encouraging where my writing is concerned, while my sisters Jen and Claire have rendered such care to our aging mother as has eased my own mind considerably, and freed me to labor at such projects as this one. Ashley Smith, of Cleveland, Ohio, a Presbyterian elder who works with the Cleveland Youth Orchestra, Karen Smith of Oakmont, Pennsylvania, a frequent soprano soloist, and her mother (and Ashley's grandmother), Betty Hicks, a lifelong organist, have joined in or initiated numerous discussions of worship through the years, and one is ever mindful of key considerations in light thereof. Of course, I am most grateful that the Lord saw fit to bring me into the world through, and place me in the care of, two of the most loving and gracious parents a child could ever hope for: my mother, Dorothy Herrick Slemmons, and my late father, Robert

Sheldon Slemmons. I continually give thanks, and I do so again now, that my parents raised us in the church: Sunday school, worship, youth choir, bell choir, youth groups, etc., every week whenever each was in session.

Finally, I give thanks for Victoria, for whom worship is, not just theory but in reality, the most joyous daily activity. She has graciously borne with me through the years in my labors on *Year D* and repeatedly confirmed its merits. I bless the Lord for her ministry of prayer, in song, and at the harp, for the sweetness of her voice and her spirit, and for the lovely sounds of her inspired psalm settings, to say nothing of all the other dimensions of the life of Christian marriage and friendship that we share in Christ. Nevertheless, *Come, Lord Jesus!*

PART I

The Christmas Cycle
Advent—Christmas—Epiphany

First Sunday of Advent

Jeremiah 33:14–16

Psalm 25:1–10

1 Thessalonians 3:9–13

Luke 21:25–36

In Preparation for Worship

God of Creation, who established the sun, the moon and the stars,
when these are darkened, help us to stand by your grace.
Spirit of revelation, who set the limits of the earth and the seas,
when these are shaken, help us to stand with your grace.
Son of Man, who comes with the clouds, when the worries of this life
threaten to entrap us, help us to stand in your grace.

Call to Worship

Lift up your souls to the Lord, O people!
Place all your trust in God!
> **The Lord is our righteousness!**
> **Our God instructs sinners in the way to obey.**

O Lord, do not remember the sins of your people!
May those who call on you never be put to shame!
> **The Lord is our righteousness!**
> **Our God leads the humble in faithfulness.**

Keep the commands of the Lord, O people!
Remember your people in your mercy, O Lord!
> **The Lord is our righteousness!**
> **Praise God, who is our truth and salvation!**

Opening Prayer

God of truth and righteousness, we turn to you in anticipation of your coming to bring justice and peace into our world. Strengthen our hearts in holiness, unite us with our neighbors in love, direct our way along your righteous paths and among your righteous people of every time and place, that we may be found blameless at your return.

Call to Confession

Do not let yourselves be weighed down by the waste and the worries of this world. Such are not the will of God, but the ways of a world that is perishing in sin. The will of God is that we hope in Jesus Christ to strengthen us to resist and escape the snares of this world, and to speak a word of grace in response to our sin, giving us confidence to stand in the Day of Judgment. Let us confess our sin.

Prayer of Confession

God of hope, we confess that we are often lacking in faith, quickly seizing upon what seem to be reasons for despair. We are constantly coming up short on faith, hope, and love, and we blame others for it. When will we remember that no one desires our freedom and our joy more than you? Forgive us, O God, and strengthen our hearts in holiness, that we might remember all the reasons we have for hoping in your coming to us once again.

Declaration of Forgiveness

When the powers of the heavens are shaken, those who wait for God are to lift up their heads and know that redemption is drawing near. Do not be weighed down by guilt any longer, but enjoy the lightness of your new freedom from sin. Know the simple joy of being taught the ways of obedience, in the full assurance that you are forgiven in Christ Jesus.

Presentation of Tithes and Offerings

Our giving to God is an act of hope, a public proclamation of our trust that the future and the church both belong to Jesus Christ. When heaven and earth have passed away, only the words of the living Word will remain. God has given us everything in Jesus Christ, the living Word. What shall we offer in return?

Prayer of Dedication

Eternal God, let us be counted among the givers.
Catch us in the act of giving.
Accept these gifts of our devotion,
move with them hard, craggy hearts, and stir the mighty ocean
with your faith and hope and love, in the light of which we give them.

The Charge

Be awake and ever on the lookout
for signs of our creating and re-creating God.
Be awake and ever open to signs of hope
in the coming of Christ.
Be awake and ever willing to obey the Spirit of holiness and love.
Strengthen one another when faith is lacking.
Encourage those lost in despair.
Increase in love for one and all,
for it is God's will that you do these things.

Second Sunday of Advent

Malachi 3:1–4

Luke 1:68–79

Philippians 1:3–11

Luke 3:1–6

In Preparation for Worship

Holy God, you began a work in me in my baptism into Christ.
By your kindness you allow this work to go on
through the forgiveness of my sins.
Thank you for inviting me
to be your partner in your new creation.
Here I am, O Lord, repentant of former ways,
ready and waiting to create with you and to be re-created by you.

Call to Worship

We share in the grace of God together.
> Let us prepare for a harvest of righteousness,
> and choose the ways of God, who refines us as pure silver.

We share in the tender mercies of our loving God.
> Let us overflow with love for the Lord
> and for all those whom God has called to repentance.

We share in the righteous work of worshiping our God.
> Let us serve the Lord our Savior without fear,
> our God who guides us in the way of peace.

Opening Prayer

Saving God, you have chosen priests and prophets to prepare your people to receive forgiveness of sins and to proclaim salvation to all the world. We have seen your light shining in the darkness. We have heard your voice calling in the wilderness. We seek to be your servant people, defenders of the gospel of our Lord Jesus Christ, in whose name we pray.

Call to Confession

God has issued the call! Prepare for the coming of the Lord! Let everyone be bathed in the light of repentance! Let all turn their lives to God and receive the gift of forgiveness. In this way, all flesh shall see the salvation of God. Let us confess our sins to God, and welcome the gracious Spirit of Christ into our hearts.

Prayer of Confession

God of Peace, through your servant John, you have called us to be a penitent people and to make way for your coming into our dry, desolate lives. Yet we forestall repentance, stubbornly refusing to change our ways, which are not your ways. We ask not only your abiding grace and mercy, already given in Jesus Christ, but we also ask the courage to practice the deep peace of turning to you, treasuring your very own Spirit within our hearts, so that we might serve you faithfully as have the saints before us.

Declaration of Forgiveness

The One who has begun a good work in you will surely bring it to completion! Trust that the grace of the Lord greets you each time you turn around to seek your God! Now may love overflow in you, and pour forth from you—love for the One who will raise you up, pure and blameless, in the day of Jesus Christ. Know that you are saved through your repentance and by the forgiveness of your sins.

Presentation of the Tithes and Offerings

Let your offerings be purified and refined.
Let them be offered with clean and contrite hearts.
Let them be made in righteousness and love.
Let us render our blessings to the Lord.

Prayer of Dedication

God of grace,
we lift up this humble harvest for your blessing,
praying that you might judge it a harvest of righteousness.
Pour forth your Spirit upon these gifts and upon these givers,
that all your people might be given insight into their godly use,
to the glory and praise of our Savior, Jesus Christ,
in whose name we pray.

Charge and Blessing

Be ever in thanksgiving,
for the sharing you have in the gospel of Jesus.
Be ever in humility,
that the joy of the Spirit might reside with you.
Be ever in prayer,
and God's longing for you will break upon you
like the light of dawn.

Third Sunday of Advent

Zephaniah 3:14–20
Isaiah 12:2–6
Philippians 4:4–7
Luke 3:7–18

In Preparation for Worship

I lift my heart to you in both
joyless and joyful circumstances.
I seek my peace in you, though I do not understand your peace.
I ask that you would guard my heart and cleanse my mind,
that the purest prayers of thanks may rise
in praise of you for your very nearness.

Call to Worship

Surely God is our salvation!
The Lord is our strength and our might!
>   **We will trust in the Lord.**
>   **We will not be afraid.**

Give thanks to the Lord!
Call upon the holy name of God!
>   **We will tell the nations of the works of God!**
>   **We will exalt God's holy name!**

Sing praises for all God's glorious deeds!
Make them known to all the earth!
>   **We will shout aloud and sing for joy!**
>   **For the Great and Holy One of Israel is in our midst!**

Opening Prayer

Redeeming God,
through even the most terrible judgment,
you preserve your people to be a faithful remnant
and you command us to rejoice in our salvation with all our hearts.
We will not be afraid as long as you are in our midst,
for you are the Lord, our Savior,
who restores the fortunes of the faithful.
In you we rejoice!

Call to Confession

The God of Israel is in your midst, the Lord,
who takes away the judgments against you.
Do not fear disaster or judgment, but fear only the holiness of the Lord.
In confession of our sin, let us acknowledge God's wonderful grace
and mighty holiness, that we might find shelter in the peace of the Lord.

Prayer of Confession

Righteous God,
we confess that we have not produced fruits worthy of repentance,
but we have filled our lives with chaff and dust.
We are sinners in need of your holy baptism, not just of water,
but of your Holy Spirit and purifying fire.
We turn to you now,
for you are our only hope of bearing good fruit and doing justice.
Forgive us, O Lord, and fill us with your grace.

Declaration of Forgiveness

Do not fear, O people. But let your shame be turned into praise and disaster be taken away from you, so that you will not bear reproach. God has turned away your enemies, that you may prosper in the land. Christ is our Lord, who gives victory over judgment, who rejoices with gladness over all who turn to God, who renews you in his love. From now on, live in his peace.

Presentation of the Tithes and Offerings

The Lord is near! Let us rejoice in God's presence, forsaking all our anxieties, and drawing water from the wellspring of salvation. Do not worry about anything, but in everything give thanks to God. Let us render our thank offerings to God.

Prayer of Dedication

God of the Sabbath,
we offer you our best, our first,
our peace, our rest.
We ask your grace to fill us and protect us,
to restore us and redirect us
in the proper use of these blessings.
May they advance your peace,
testify to your love,
and give you joy, in the name of Jesus.

The Charge

Separate what is holy and fruitful in your life
from whatever is unholy and fruitless,
and be filled with the Spirit of purity!
Bear fruit worthy of repentance and rejoice in your rescuer,
who is Christ Jesus the Lord!
Be mindful of your Creator who is always in your midst,
and make all your requests known to God
with thanksgiving and with peace.

Fourth Sunday of Advent

Micah 5:2–5a

Luke 1:47–55 OR Psalm 80:1–7

Hebrews 10:5–10

Luke 1:39–40 (46–55)

IN PREPARATION FOR WORSHIP

O God of Peace,
from ancient days you have called us
to return to you, to live securely, to live in peace;
you have labored long to bring yourself to life
within our very hearts and minds.
And so we gather as your flock, for you to feed us
in the majesty of your name.

CALL TO WORSHIP

Hear us, O Shepherd of Israel!
You who are enthroned upon the wings of angels!
> **Stir up your might and come to save us!**

O LORD God of hosts,
how long will you be angry with the prayers of your people?
> **Restore us, O God! Let your face shine, that we may be saved!**

How long will you feed us with the bread of tears?
How long will you give us tears to drink in full measure?
> **Restore us, O God! Let your face shine, that we may be saved!**

Fourth Sunday of Advent 13

Opening Prayer

Atoning God, you have neither desired nor taken any pleasure in sacrifices and burnt offerings, but in Jesus Christ you have put an end to them once and for all, and established your holy will as our way of sanctification. We rejoice in your condemnation of sin and evil, and in your victory over all forms of oppression and pride. May our souls magnify you, O Lord! May our spirits rejoice in Christ our Savior!

Call to Confession

The Lord regards the meek and lowly, and humbles the proud and haughty. The Lord brings down the powerful, but fills the poor with good things. The mercy of God is for those who revere and would magnify the Lord. Therefore, let us humble ourselves, remembering to God that we are ever in need of the mercy which is promised to all who fear God. Let us confess our sin.

Prayer of Confession

God of Justice and Mercy,
we confess that we have filled the hunger
and the emptiness in our lives
with the things of this world.
We have forgotten that all good things come from you,
we have sought satisfaction elsewhere,
and we have come up empty.
Forgive us for our proud thoughts,
our vain desires,
and our lack of trust in you.
Remember your mercy toward your lowly servants.

Declaration of Forgiveness

God remembers the mercy promised to our ancestors in the faith, and in conforming to the will of God, Jesus Christ has fulfilled God's promise of mercy. Likewise, let us conform our living under the rule of mercy to the will of God. You are made holy by Christ's offering his body on your behalf. Now live as God's holy and forgiven people. Blessed are all those who believe the promises of God.

Presentation of Tithes and Offerings

The Lord remembers the ancient promises and commitments made to our ancestors and has kept his promises from generation to generation. Let us remember and keep our commitments to the Lord on behalf of those who come after us. Let us bless with our gifts the Lord who has so richly blessed us.

Prayer of Dedication

Mighty God, you fill our lives with countless good things, and you favor all those who fear you. In gratitude for your goodness to us, and in awe of your power and willingness to bless, we lift up these humble gifts to be used according to your holy will, that our lives and our living, our gifts and our giving, might magnify your blessed name.

Charge and Blessing

Rejoice in the Lord, and let the face of God shine upon.
Rejoice in the Lord, and let the salvation of Christ lift up your soul.
Rejoice in the Lord. Again I say, rejoice,
  and let the Holy Spirit fill your hearts with praise to the living God!

Christmas, First Proper (ABC)
Christmas Eve

Isaiah 9:2–7
Psalm 96
Titus 2:11–14
Luke 2:1–14 (15–20)

IN PREPARATION FOR WORSHIP

Wrapped in cloth and laid in a manger,
for there was nowhere else for you to rest.
Such was the humble state of your birth.
Yet an angel of the Lord announced it
and the shining glory of the Lord revealed it,
and those who heard and saw it were terrified.
Such was the majesty of the divine declaration.
But the angel said, *Do not be afraid;*
for it is good news of great joy for all:
a Savior, a sign; glory, peace, and favor!
Holy God, we marvel at what the angels said and sang,
at what the shepherds heard and told,
at what Mary treasured and pondered in her heart.
But above all, we are amazed at you,
and your wonderful ways among us.

CALL TO WORSHIP

The grace of God that brings salvation has appeared to all people!
> **It teaches us to say "no" to sin and ungodliness,**
> **and to live upright and godly lives.**

We gather to wait for the blessed hope and the manifestation
of the glory of our great God and Savior, Jesus Christ!
> **It is Christ who comes for us, and has given himself to us**
> **so that he might redeem us from all iniquity,**
> **and purify for himself a people of his own**
> **who are zealous for good deeds.**

Let us direct our thoughts to Bethlehem and recall what has taken place, that which the Lord has made known to us.
> **Let us glorify and praise our God**
> **for all that we have seen and heard!**

Opening Prayer [Psalm 96]

O Lord, you are sovereign! We declare it that heaven and earth may hear it! We come to adore you in your holy splendor, to ascribe glory to your name, to render offerings and sing anew of your gospel of salvation. You are great, O Lord, and greatly to be praised. Come, O God, and speak your truth in righteousness. Show us your presence that we may exult and rejoice in your courts, and tell of your salvation from day to day.

Call to Confession [Titus 2:11–14]

With the revealing of God's grace in Jesus Christ, the offer of salvation is extended to all who receive him. Meanwhile, we await a further and final revelation of the glory of our Savior. Assured of his grace and hopeful of his return, let us confess our sins, that by renouncing worldly impiety, we might avail ourselves of Christ's sanctifying work and be newly fashioned into the people God calls us to be: upright, reverent, and zealous for good deeds.

Prayer of Confession [Psalm 96]

O Lord our God who made the heavens and the earth, you are to be revered above all gods! The gods of the peoples are mere idols, yet we confess we too have allowed ourselves to be distracted and deceived by them, and failed to ascribe to you the glory that is your due. Forgive us, O God, for every idolatrous impulse, every selfish act, every iniquity, every joyless failure to make room for you and for the Christ whom you sent to save us and teach us the way of peace. Fill us anew with the joy of your salvation and with confidence that all your judgments are true and just and altogether praiseworthy. In Jesus' name we pray.

Christmas, First Proper (ABC)—Christmas Eve

Declaration of Forgiveness [Isaiah 9:2–7]

Where the deep darkness of sin covered the land, now a great light is shining. God in Christ has broken the yoke of our burden, the bar on our shoulders, the rod of the oppressor; for the Son of God has been born for us and authority rests upon his shoulders. The authority of the Prince of Peace shall grow continually; by him we are forgiven and set free, and there shall be endless peace for those who belong to his kingdom. Know that in Christ Jesus we are forgiven and set at liberty to live in peace.

Presentation of Tithes and Offerings

The world is firmly established; it shall never be moved. Such is the steadfast love and faithfulness of God toward the whole creation. Therefore, let us make offerings to the Lord and dedicate them to the ministry of Christ, in order that God's marvelous deeds might be declared and the honor and majesty of Jesus Christ might be loudly proclaimed to this generation.

Prayer of Dedication

We bless you, Almighty God, Everlasting Father, for your marvelous and merciful provision; for sending us your Son to reign as the Prince of Peace and your Spirit to serve as our Wonderful Counsellor. We join our voices with the heavenly hosts to extol you, and we rejoice that you have decreed such blessing and favor, such grace and mercy for your people through the gift of Jesus Christ. Receive now these gifts, we pray, that your wisdom might direct their use, your power might render them effective, and your will might be done in the life of your church; in Jesus' name.

The Blessing

May the ancient gospel of the gift of Jesus
fill your hearts with new songs of praise.
May the good news of great joy
inspire your thoughts of the God of grace.
May the glory of the Lord flood the world
with peace on earth as you go forth in the name of Christ,
glorifying and praising God.

Christmas, Second Proper (ABC)
Christmas Morning

Isaiah 62:6–12
Psalm 97
Titus 3:4–7
Luke 2:(1–7) 8–20

In Preparation for Worship

So high are you, what creature can reach you?
So merciful are you, you come within reach.
Indeed, you dam the very sources of sin,
and become the fresh fountainhead for all that is human.
O Christ, let your Spirit of renewal and rebirth
wash over your people and give us new life.

Call to Worship [see Psalm 97]

Tremble, O mountains, at the presence of the Lord.
>**The sovereign Lord lights up the world!**
>**His lightnings break through the clouds and thick darkness.**

Bow down, you gods, before the Creator of all the earth!
>**The Lord, the most high, is far above all gods!**
>**His judgments resound throughout the heavens!**

Behold, O people, the glory of the Lord!
>**With the dawn comes joy in the hearts of the righteous!**
>**Rejoice, O earth, and give thanks to his holy name!**

Christmas, Second Proper (ABC)— Christmas Morning

OPENING PRAYER [see Luke 2:1–20; Isaiah 62:6]

O LORD our God, who made with David an eternal covenant and fulfilled that promise in the city that bears his name: the news of your Son's birth for us is good and glorious news, indeed! As we remember and consider it anew, let it bring to our hearts such joy and gladness that we might never be silent concerning the glory of your humble presence among us, your grace that gives us hope, and your peace and favor that inspire us, and the whole host of heaven, to sing to you songs of praise everlasting.

CALL TO CONFESSION [Titus 3:4–7]

The goodness and lovingkindness of God our Savior has appeared for our salvation, not because we have earned it, but because of the greatness of God's mercy and the depth of our need. Therefore, emboldened by the Holy Spirit, who has been richly and graciously poured out upon us for the sake of our rectification, let us confess our sin and give voice to our hope of eternal life, the very life which those who trust in Jesus stand to inherit with him, who is heir of all things.

PRAYER OF CONFESSION [Psalm 97:3, 7, 10]

Sovereign LORD, your righteousness and justice are a consuming fire, in the light of which those who worship lifeless images and boast in worthless idols are exposed for their shameful ways. We confess that we too have misdirected our worship, misplaced our trust, and sought security in the things of this world. Forgive us, O God, and inspire us with such righteous revulsion at the prospect of sin, temptation, and evil that we might be ever more assured of your love and mercy; for surely in Christ Jesus you have rescued us from the ways of the wicked, and you regard those who are faithful as you regard Christ himself, with whom you are well pleased.

DECLARATION OF FORGIVENESS [Isaiah 62:10–12]

The LORD has proclaimed to the ends of the earth, and yes, to daughter Zion, "Your salvation comes!" God comes and his reward is with him; for you are the holy people of God, those whom the LORD has redeemed. And you shall be called, "A City Sought Out and Not Forsaken." Go through its gates and make way for the people! Build up the highway and clear it of stones. For Christ himself is a sign for the peoples, a sign of God's redeeming love, by whose grace and mercy we are forgiven and restored.

Presentation of Tithes and Offerings [Isaiah 62:7–9]

Remind the Lord and take no rest until he establishes Jerusalem and makes it renowned throughout the earth! For the Lord has sworn by his right hand and by his mighty arm: "I will not again give your grain as food for your enemies, and foreigners shall not drink the wine for which you have labored; but those who garner it shall eat it and praise the Lord, and those who gather it shall drink it in my holy courts." With such promises of provision for the people of God, surely we are free to devote what we have to the mission of God: that those outside the fellowship of faith might hear the good news of God's gift of salvation, turn to Jesus, and, through the power of the Spirit, be joined to the body of Christ. To this end, let us offer our gifts.

Prayer of Dedication

Lord Jesus, in the humble circumstances of your birth, we see the extent of your descent on your merciful errand of redemption; placed in a manger, as though mere forage for lowly beasts, your vulnerability discloses your love for the poor and the weak; your purity divulges your majesty, inspires adoration, and calls us to responsibility. May these offerings be blessed and used in the same spirit, for the same redeeming aim that brought you to Bethlehem as a babe and led you to the place of your complete surrender and our liberation.

The Charge and Blessing

Let the mountains and hills, the fields and the plains,
the coastlands and islands ring with the news
that the Lord Jesus Christ is born to be king!
Let all rejoice who long for him to correct
the corruption of the world, to judge its injustice.
For the favor of the Lord our God is seen
in the gift of Christ Jesus to rule and reign.
Go in his power as bearers of the good news.
Go in his name to proclaim his peace.

Christmas, Third Proper (ABC)
Christmas Day

Isaiah 52:7–10
Psalm 98
Hebrews 1:1–4 (5–12)
John 1:1–14

IN PREPARATION FOR WORSHIP

O Lord our Sovereign,
your faithfulness is sure,
your majesty glorious,
your marvelous deeds worthy of praise.
Above all, your gracious revelation
of your mercy in Jesus Christ
is the source of our future hope!
May the good news of your incarnate Word
so impress us with the fullness of your love and truth,
that we would burst forth with joyful songs of adoration and praise;
in Jesus' name.

CALL TO WORSHIP

The vindication of the LORD is revealed
in the sight of the nations.
> **Let us sing of the victory of our God,**
> **for the LORD has done marvelous things.**
God has spoken to us by the Son, Jesus Christ,
the Word of God in human flesh.

> **Let us praise Christ the Lord,**
> **the perfect reflection of the glory of God,**
> **who sustains all things by his powerful word!**
> Make a joyful noise to the Lord, all the earth.
> Break forth into joyous song and sing praises!
> **Let us worship in the light of God,**
> **for the light of God is Jesus Christ**
> **through whom all things come to life.**

Opening Prayer

Holy God, source of all life and light and love, as your Word was with you in the beginning and took part fully in the birth of creation, so it is in the renewal of our human nature. The divine Word became human, your Son was born in the flesh, that he might give us new life and the light of saving faith. Therefore, let your Word speak to and work among us now, that we might be true witnesses to your glory, and the glory of your Son, Jesus Christ, who lives and reigns with you, one God, now and forever.

Call to Confession [Psalm 98:7–9]

Creation rejoices: the sea roars, the floods clap their hands, the hills sing together for joy at the presence of the Lord, who is coming to judge the earth with righteousness, and the peoples with equity. Let us therefore confess our sins, and thus prepare for his coming, that we too, when we meet the Lord face to face, might receive him with joy.

Prayer of Confession [John 1:9–14]

Eternal God, you have sent your Word as light for the whole world, yet we confess that the world has not known him, and we ourselves, who belong to Christ, have failed to accept all that he would reveal to us. Forgive us, O God, for our sin, shortsightedness, and stubbornness. Show us anew the glory of your Son, the One full of grace and truth, that we may receive more of his nature and avail ourselves of the new life, the new birth, and the eternal fellowship he offers to those who believe in his name; indeed, it is in Jesus' name that we pray.

Declaration of Forgiveness [John 1:5; Isaiah 52:7–10]

The light of Christ shines in the darkness and the darkness cannot overcome it. The Lord has comforted his people; he has redeemed Jerusalem. Break forth together into singing; lift up your voices and sing for joy at the return of the Lord, for all the ends of the earth shall see the salvation of our God. In the name of Jesus Christ, I declare to you salvation and peace, for your God reigns!

Presentation of Tithes and Offerings

Through Christ, the appointed heir of all things, we are likewise heirs of God. In Christ, the Son through whom the worlds were created, we are likewise children of God! With such grace as we have known in Jesus Christ, let us live according to his self-giving ways, and offer our gifts and our hearts to God.

Prayer of Dedication

God of glory, what a wonderful gift is your Son to this world! Jesus Christ, the precise imprint of your being, he who sustains all things by his word, has by his complete surrender made purification for sins on our behalf! Mindful, therefore, of his supreme offering, we offer these expressions of our love and thanks, that in your wisdom you might use them according to your redeeming purpose, for your glory and joy, in Jesus' name.

The Blessing

Go forth bearing the excellent name of Jesus!
And may the majesty on high attend you,
the presence of Christ fill you with joy,
and the Spirit inspire you with songs of devotion
and words of praise.

First Sunday after Christmas

1 Samuel 2:18–20, 26

Psalm 148

Colossians 3:12–17

Luke 2:41–52

IN PREPARATION FOR WORSHIP

You call us into your heart of peace,
into one thankful body, into one holy love.
Therefore, we clothe ourselves with love,
with compassion, kindness, humility, and meekness,
with patience, peace, and forgiveness,
all for you, all for you.

CALL TO WORSHIP

Praise the LORD in the highest heavens!
Praise the LORD, you heavenly hosts!
> **We praise the name of the LORD, our Creator!**
> **For God commanded and the world was created.**

Praise the LORD, O sun and moon!
Praise the LORD, you shining stars!
> **We praise the name of the LORD our God!**
> **For the glory of God is over heaven and earth.**

Praise the LORD, O people of the earth!
Let all who trust in the LORD, praise the LORD!
> **God has raised up victory for the faithful!**
> **Draw near to us, Almighty God, as we draw near to you.**

Opening Prayer

God of our salvation,
who calls us into the one body of Christ:
may the word of Christ dwell in us richly;
may the peace of Christ rule in our hearts;
may the love of Christ clothe us
and bind us together in perfect harmony,
that our worship might render all thanks and glory to you!

Call to Confession

Let all adopt an attitude of humility and meekness,
bearing with one another in peace.
For God has limited every creature,
and all are in need of forgiveness and grace.
Let us confess our sins to God,
whose name alone is to be exalted.

Prayer of Confession

God of grace, we admit that we have been quick to complain but slow to forgive, short on wisdom and long on foolishness, eager to wander and wanting in gratitude for all that you have given us. Forgive us our divisiveness and disunity. Guide us with your holy teaching. Raise us in your ways of wisdom. Grow us into the full stature of Christ Jesus our Lord.

Declaration of Forgiveness

Be thankful! Let gratitude give rise to songs in your hearts!
Forgive one another as God in Christ has forgiven you.
Truly, you have been called to peace.
Therefore, be at peace with God and one another.

Presentation of Tithes and Offerings

How slow we are to comprehend the nearness of God, the wisdom of Jesus, the presence of the Holy Spirit teaching us and questioning us with the truth! How cluttered are our hearts, filled as they are with the false treasures of this world! Would that we might clear away the perishable goods that we have assembled there, put them to redeeming use, and make room for our true and everlasting treasure, who alone is worthy of our inner devotion, and every outward act of faith.

Prayer of Dedication

Let your name alone be exalted, O God! For you have created all things in heaven, on earth, and in the great, wide deep. It is only right that we commit these treasures to the praise of your glory. For indeed all of creation praises you! Receive our offering of gratitude and love, for we trust that we are ever close to your heart. May you draw ever nearer to ours, even as Christ matures within us daily.

The Charge and Blessing

Hold fast to your place among the people of God!
Dwell on the wonders of the living Word!
Give yourselves to growth in the things of the Spirit,
and may the favor of God rest upon you forevermore.

Second Sunday after Christmas (ABC)

Jeremiah 31:7–14

Psalm 147:12–20

Ephesians 1:3–14

John 1:(1–9) 10–18

In Preparation for Worship

We gather to your good pleasure,
to hear your holy word of truth,
to praise you for your glorious grace,
freely bestowed upon us in Christ Jesus.
Seal us with your Holy Spirit, mark us for your service,
as you have ordained it, O blessed God.

Call to Worship

Sing aloud with gladness! Shout for the chief of nations!
Proclaim, give praise, and say,
> "Save, O Lord, your chosen people!
> May our mourning be turned into joy!"

The Lord shall gather them all together:
the blind, the lame, and those in labor.
> "Save, O Lord, your chosen people!
> May our mourning be turned into joy!"

A great company shall return to the Lord.
God will shepherd them with great consolation.
> O women, rejoice with dancing!
> O men, make merry in your hearts!
> For the Lord has blessed us abundantly!

Opening Prayer

Holy God, you fulfill all things in accordance with your holy will. You have sent your Word among us. You have lavished grace upon us. You have redeemed us by the blood of Jesus Christ, the Beloved, and our eternal Lord. Consecrate us for lives of service and empower us with the Holy Spirit, all to the praise of your glory.

Call to Confession

From the fullness of Jesus Christ we have received grace upon grace.
Through Christ we have redemption and forgiveness,
but not without the cost of Christ's very own blood.
In an act of contrite confession, let us repent of the sin
by which we compound the sufferings of our Lord.

Prayer of Confession

God of Grace and Truth, you shine your eternal light into the darkness of our fallen world, and yet we often fail to comprehend it. Your eternal Word speaks to us every day, yet we fail to accept Christ fully. Therefore, we humble ourselves before you, praying that you would free us once again from sin, raise us up into the radiant beams of your glory, and gather us into closer fellowship with Christ, in whose name we pray.

Declaration of Forgiveness

The Lord has paid the ransom for captive Israel, and Christ Jesus has paid the ransom for you! God promises to lead in a straight path all those who are willing to follow. To all who accept this testimony of grace and truth, embodied in Jesus Christ, the Word made flesh, God gives the power to be children of God, born of the very Spirit of God. Accept this Word. Accept this grace. Accept your new birth and begin your life anew this day!

Presentation of Tithes and Offerings

Praise the Lord! For our God alone grants true prosperity and lasting peace within! The Lord alone blesses your children and fills you with the finest of wheat! The Lord alone is your source of strength and the everlasting Word revealed to you in Christ! Let us praise God for the glorious grace that has been bestowed upon us in the Beloved. Let us gather up a harvest of joy to express our love of Christ, even as, in the fullness of time, we too will be gathered up!

Prayer of Dedication

Blessed are you, O God and Father of our Lord Jesus Christ! For you have blessed us in Christ with every spiritual blessing in heaven and marked us with the seal of the promised Holy Spirit as a pledge of our inheritance toward redemption as your people! Therefore, all that we have and all that we are belong to you. May our words, our works, our living and our giving add to the glory of your name!

The Charge and Blessing

Trust in the name of Jesus Christ, the eternal Word of God made flesh!
Receive the power of the Holy Spirit, and be born anew!
Come alive in the triune God!

Epiphany (ABC)

Isaiah 60:1–6

Psalm 72:1–7, 10–14

Ephesians 3:1–12

Matthew 2:1–12

In Preparation for Worship

O Lord, we gather, old and young;
we seek you, O radiant One, from near and far away.
Arise and shine; show us your glory,
that the nations may come to your light
and those who govern to the brightness of your dawn.
For you have pity on the weak and the needy;
you save those who suffer oppression and violence,
and you regard all your children as precious in your sight.
We bless you, O God, for manifesting your glorious reign
in Jesus Christ your Son.

Call to Worship

From Bethlehem has come a ruler
to shepherd God's people.
> **Let us bring our costly gifts,**
> **and proclaim the praise of the Lord.**

The light of heaven leads the way,
just as God promised through the prophets of old.
> **We will rejoice in the presence**
> **of the Son of God, born king of the Jews.**

Come and consider the mystery of Christ!
Come and share in the promises of God!
> **Let all rulers and kings fall down before him!**
> **Let all nations give him service.**

OPENING PRAYER [Ephesians 3:8–12]

O God our Creator, your plan for redemption, once hidden for ages, you have now revealed in Jesus Christ, and you have commissioned your church to make your wisdom known in all its variety to the rulers and authorities in the heavenly places. For such is your eternal purpose that you carry out in Christ Jesus our Lord, so that we might approach you with boldness and confidence through him, interceding for the nations and declaring the gracious news of the boundless riches in Christ. Therefore, we pray that the worship we offer here and now, and the service we will render in future, wherever your Spirit leads us, would serve this great end, for your glory and good pleasure, in the name of Jesus Christ.

CALL TO CONFESSION [Psalm 72:1–2]

To the sovereign Christ is given all authority to administer justice and righteousness for the weak, the poor, and the oppressed, including those oppressed and driven by the power of sin. Since we have confidence to approach God with boldness through faith in Jesus Christ, let us confess our sin and seek the freedom, absolution, and deliverance that Christ alone can give.

PRAYER OF CONFESSION

Our Lord Jesus Christ, yours is the light that draws people from every corner of the world. Though darkness blankets the earth and blinds us to untold evil and even to our own sins, your light reveals who we are, what we have done and failed to do, everything of which we are ashamed. Forgive us, O Christ, and lead us into your radiant presence, freed, exonerated, and unashamed of the past. Bathe us in your light, and fill the world with your glory, that we may thrill and rejoice with you at the streaming of the nations to worship you at your throne.

Declaration of Forgiveness [Isaiah 60:1–6]

As the Lord has said to the sovereign Son of God, "Arise, shine; for your light has come," so the glory of the Lord has risen upon those who belong to Christ Jesus and believe in his name. Arise from the valleys of doubt and despair; shine with the dawn of Christ reflected in your eyes. Let the glory of his grace be borne on your shoulders, resound in your speech, and reverberate in your songs, as you are forgiven and refreshed for the life of faith, lived in his service as his body the church.

Presentation of Tithes and Offerings [Ephesians 3:8–12]

God has resolved from eternity to make the fullness of his wisdom known through the church, the sovereign wisdom revealed in Jesus Christ our Lord. Therefore, in keeping faith with Christ, let us offer and dedicate our gifts for the service of God's eternal purpose.

Prayer of Dedication [Ephesians 3:7; Matthew 2:12]

Gracious God, who has blessed us with many gifts and graces, may these offerings be used in the service of your gospel and made effective by the power at work in your Holy Spirit; and as those who first followed the star to worship your Son departed by a different way, may we too have our courses changed for the good in accordance with your wisdom and will; in Jesus' name.

The Blessing

May the glory of the Lord revealed in Jesus
inspire the testimony of the church in mission
and fill each heart with exceeding joy!
Go in peace and in the power of the Spirit
to share the rich promise of the gospel of Christ.

First Sunday after Epiphany
Ordinary Time 1 (*Baptism of the Lord*)

Isaiah 43:1–7
Psalm 29
Acts 8:14–17
Luke 3:15–17, 21–22

In Preparation for Worship

Almighty Father,
you are a God of new beginnings!
Let your voice go out across the waters,
let it thunder even unto me,
let it speak your kingdom into being
as we adore the Christ in glory!

Call to Worship

The voice of the Lord is over the waters.
The God of glory thunders with power and majesty!
> **Give glory to God!**
> **Worship the Lord of glory and strength!**

The voice of the Lord breaks the cedars.
The voice of God makes the oaks to whirl and strips the forest bare!
> **Give glory to God!**
> **Let all in the temple of the Lord cry, "Glory!"**

The voice of the Lord flashes with fire!
The voice of God shakes the wilderness!
> **O God of glory, O God of strength,**
> **bless us with your peace!**

Opening Prayer

Mighty God, who sits enthroned over the waters,
you are our Ruler forever and ever!
With the element of water cleanse and refresh us.
With the element of fire refine and prove us.
With the Spirit of your baptism claim us for your own,
and make us one with your Son and our Savior,
in the one baptism which we share.

Call to Confession

God says to the north, "Give them up," and to the south, "Do not withold my sons and daughters from me, but bring them from the ends of the earth! For you are precious in my sight, and honored, and I love you!" Should we not, then, prepare ourselves for coming home to our God? We do so in the cleansing act of confession.

Prayer of Confession

**Creator God,
though you yourself have created us,
we confess that we have failed to trust in you as we should.
We fear, though you have told us we should not.
We doubt, when you would have us believe.
We hide, when you would gather us to yourself in love.
We hoard, when you would have us share.
Redeem us, Lord.
Call us each by name,
that we might return to you in joy
and fall at your feet once again.**

Declaration of Forgiveness

The LORD our God, the Holy One of Israel, is our Savior! God has ransomed you, saying, "I give people in return for you, nations in exchange for your life. Do not fear, for I have redeemed you. Do not fear, for I am with you." Christ Jesus has paid the full and final ransom to buy us back from our enslavement to sin and our failure to yield good fruit. As the chaff is consumed, so let yourselves be gathered to God in thanksgiving as a joyful harvest of the finest of wheat.

Presentation of Tithes and Offerings

We have been created to glorify God! Therefore, let your stewardship as disciples of Jesus reflect not only your baptism with water, but your baptism in the Holy Spirit, that the love and generosity with which you give will testify to the gracious outpouring of God's own Spirit. Let us give with joy, thanksgiving, and love, inspired by the knowledge that the baptism in which we all share is none other than the baptism of Christ, indeed, that we share with him in all things!

Prayer of Dedication

Lord, you are a God of whom we have come to expect great things, though they are often disguised in simple elements, subtle situations, humble circumstances. Sanctify, we pray, these few provisions and prepare them for your mighty purpose, that they too might testify to your sovereignty over our lives and over all your creation.

The Charge and Blessing

Live in Christ as Christ lives in you!
Receive the anointing of the Holy Spirit!
Surely, you too shall see heaven opened
and know the pleasure of God!

Second Sunday after Epiphany
Ordinary Time 2

Isaiah 62:1–5

Psalm 36:5–10

1 Corinthians 12:1–11

John 2:1–11

In Preparation for Worship

Your mercy reaches to the heights of heaven,
your faithfulness beyond the clouds.
Just so, we reach for you.
Your righteousness stands as true as the mountains,
your judgments are like the great deep.
Just so, we stand before you.
You shelter all your creatures, providing for them all.
Just so, we trust in you.

Call to Worship

Hear, O people, the salvation of God:
You are not forsaken. Neither is the land desolate around you.
> God has vindicated and saved us.
> The Lord delights in all the faithful.

Receive, O people, the delight of God:
The Lord is the bridegroom and you are the bride!
> The beauty of Zion shines like the dawn,
> God's people as a royal crown.

See, O people, the light of God:
With God is the fountain of life, and in the light of the LORD we see light.
> **How precious is your steadfast love, O God.**
> **Indeed, all people may take refuge in the shadow of your wings!**

Opening Prayer

You, O God, who invite us into lives of covenant and commitment,
we praise you for transforming the simple elements of our lives
into occasions for joy and cause for celebration.
Revive in us our thirst for you.
Be magnified in our minds and hearts.
Be exalted in our worship.

Call to Confession

Do not think that God judges superficially or fails to notice our false moves. The judgments of God are like the great deep and strong as the mighty mountains. Yet the selfsame God, our righteous judge, has done everything for our vindication. God has given to us the saving Christ, in whose righteousness we may take refuge and confess our sin with confidence in his enduring love and mercy.

Prayer of Confession

Holy God, you have blessed us with countless gifts
through the supreme gift of your Holy Spirit within us,
and you have charged us with sacred speech
in testimony to your goodness.
Yet we have failed to speak the pure speech of blessing
and neglected to use our gifts in accordance with your holy will.
Forgive us, O God. Renew our desire to obey you,
to reap a harvest of joy in the Spirit,
and to share with others our faith in, and our love for,
Christ Jesus, our redeeming Lord.

Declaration of Forgiveness

How precious is the steadfast love of the Lord!
How infinitely high is God's mercy!
You who trust in Christ Jesus
are not only spared the punishment of the wicked,
but you are invited to feast in the household of your Creator,
to enjoy the abundance that is found there,
and to drink from God's river of delights!
Begin anew the blessed life of faith,
and be filled with joy in the Holy Spirit!

Presentation of Tithes and Offerings

No one can say that Jesus is Lord except by the power of the Holy Spirit!
Let us then avail ourselves of the presence of the Spirit
and declare the lordship of Christ!
For Jesus is Lord over our hearts and our minds,
Lord over our loves and loyalties,
Lord over our powers and priorities,
and Lord over all we are and all we have, spirit and substance.
As you declare Jesus' lordship with your gifts,
know that the Holy Spirit is with you.

Prayer of Dedication

Take first place, Lord Jesus Christ, take first place over our lives!
You who so willingly serve your servants, be exalted among us,
and accept these gifts for use in your holy name.
May they be blessed and bring about many fruitful transformations
in accordance with your gracious and sovereign will.

The Charge and Blessing

Walk in the power of the Holy Spirit
and use your gifts for the common good.
Go in the peace of Christ Jesus the Lord
and transform fear into joy and blessing.
Live in the light of the Lord your God,
with whom is the fountain of life!

Third Sunday after Epiphany
Ordinary Time 3

Nehemiah 8:1–3, 5–6, 8–10

Psalm 19

1 Corinthians 12:12–31a

Luke 4:14–21

In Preparation for Worship

O Divine Spirit,
bring us your good news and fulfill it,
for we are poor and humble in spirit.
O Sinless Sovereign,
release us from captivity,
for we are trapped under sin and suffering.
O Light of God Eternal,
banish our blindness and help us to see,
for we seek your freedom and holy favor.

Call to Worship

Let the law and the prophets be proclaimed among the people.
> May the Holy Spirit come down and reveal them.

Do not weep, for the Spirit is here to bring good news to the poor!
> Let the poor take heart, the oppressed go free,
> the captives be released, and the blind see.

Let the people rejoice and share with those who have nothing.
For this is the year of jubilation!
> In Christ, we know the favor of God!
> The joy of the Lord shall be our strength!

Opening Prayer

Creator God, the heavens silently tell of your glory, the gentle rhythms of day and night show forth the beauty of your creation! The very words of your mouth, the holy commands of your law, are woven into your awesome, natural order! Let our ears be perfectly attentive to you, O God, that our words might become pure and reflect your purity, that our inner thoughts might be made worthy, acceptable, and pleasing in your sight, for you alone have the power to shelter and strengthen us, you alone have great power to redeem, through Jesus Christ our Lord!

Call to Confession

Those who believe in God are warned by the laws of the Lord: perfect, clear, wise, pure, enduring, true, and righteous altogether. In keeping them there is great reward! They are sweeter than honey and more desirable than gold! Yet who among us can pretend to be free from every error? In a time of confession, let us ask the Lord to clear us from our hidden and our not so hidden faults, that we might be found blameless and innocent of great transgression.

Prayer of Confession

Mighty God, in Christ you promise us freedom and forgiveness, spiritual vision and eternal salvation. Yet we have chosen to remain in the captivity of our poverty and oppression, our blindness and pessimism. As we are convicted of sin, forgive us, and convince us that we need not remain in its chains. Call us into your redeeming joy and your happy jubilee, that the world might come to see your gospel of liberation and compassion embodied, enacted, alive, and made real in our way of living, in the name and the Spirit of Christ.

Declaration of Forgiveness

Christ Jesus has conquered sin; he has endured and overcome the hostility of this world! Let there be no mistake: the righteousness of Christ is greater than your sin, greater than my sin, greater even than all our sins and those of the human race. God has even arranged the body of Christ so that the weakest members should receive the greater honor, for they manifest more than the stronger ones the total dependence on the Spirit of the Lord that pertains to one and all! Let the whole body of Christ, and each of you, the members, be strengthened and encouraged by the good news of the death of sin and the new life of Christ in you!

Presentation of Tithes and Offerings

As we are all individually members of the one body of Christ and made to drink of one Holy Spirit, let there be no dissension among us, but let each one do his or her part for the sake of the body, that all may rejoice together.

Prayer of Dedication

We humbly present these offerings, O God, and we would strive for the greater gifts! Show us your most excellent way! Bless these gifts and us as we give them, for we seek to use them in your service and bear the superior fruit of love!

The Charge and Blessing

Celebrate with joy your freedom in Christ!
Remain in Christ!
Bear with one another in love,
for love is the gift and the fruit of the Spirit
which is most pleasing to God!

Fourth Sunday after Epiphany
Ordinary Time 4

Jeremiah 1:4–10

Psalm 71:1–6

1 Corinthians 13:1–13

Luke 4:21–30

In Preparation for Worship

I come to worship the Holy One,
who took me from my mother's womb.
I come to worship the Holy One,
with power to raise from tombs of earth.
I come to worship you, Holy One,
on whom I've leaned from my lowly birth.

Call to Worship

Rescue me, O God, from the hand of the wicked,
from the grasp of the unjust and the cruel.
> **For you, O God, are my only hope,**
> **my trust, O Lord, from my youth.**

In your righteousness deliver me.
Hear my prayers and come to my aid.
> **In you, O Lord, I take refuge;**
> **let me never be put to shame.**

Be to me a safe haven and a sanctuary,
a rock of refuge and a fortress of strength.
> **For you have been with me since the day I was born;**
> **my praise is continually of you!**

Opening Prayer

God of faith and hope and love:
your love is perfect and eternal, and rejoices in the truth.
Your hope helps us endure all things.
Your faith helps us believe where we can only seek to understand.
We gather to praise you for what we know in part.
We worship you as through a mirror, dimly.
We believe in you, hope in you, love you!

Call to Confession

Be neither unaware of your limitations nor restrained by them. Bring your limitations, your sins, your failings, your faults, and your fears, and pour them out before the Lord. For God knows you better than you know yourself and continues to love you patiently, hopefully, faithfully, your sins notwithstanding. Let us confess our sins to our living, loving God.

Prayer of Confession

**Eternal God,
we confess the limits of our love;
we admit the shortness of our vision;
we own that we have been hesitant to hope and trust in you.
Humanity has corrupted the meaning of love,
while our people have broken faith with one another and with you.
Take our sins away from us, O God,
and reveal to us the kingdom
in which you would have us live.**

Declaration of Forgiveness

Friends in Christ, hear the good news of God's love:
If God is love and love keeps no record of wrongs,
then God keeps no record of wrongs.
Knowing then that you are loved by God,
believe that, in Christ, your sins go unrecorded.
Rejoice and give thanks for this forgiving love every day,
and show it to others in all that you do.

Presentation of Tithes and Offerings

We give as an act of faithfulness,
because God is eternally faithful to us.
We give as an act of hope,
because Christ is ever our reason for hope.
Yet even if we give away everything we have,
including life and limb, and have not love, there is nothing to be gained.
Therefore, let us give of ourselves and from our share of God's resources,
and do so in the spirit of love.

Prayer of Dedication

You know our minds and hearts, dear Lord.
You know our capacity for love, and our capacity for giving.
Consecrate these gifts for your use and for your glory,
even as you consecrate our act of giving, and all our living,
as expressions of your faith, hope, and love alive in us.

The Charge and Blessing

May the God who knew you before your birth
watch over you and provide.
May the Christ who calls to you to follow
go ahead of you to lead the way.
May the Spirit who stirs up love within you
fill you and flood the world with the true reality of God's perfect love.

Fifth Sunday after Epiphany
Ordinary Time 5

Isaiah 6:1–8 (9–13)
Psalm 138
1 Corinthians 15:1–11
Luke 5:1–11

In Preparation for Worship

May I never believe the good news in vain:
that you have died for my sins, O Jesus;
that you were buried in the earth;
that you are risen from the dead,
and you live again within me.
By your grace, living Lord,
you have made me what I am,
and without pretense I follow you.

Call to Worship

I give you thanks, O God, with my whole heart.
I bow down within your holy temple.
> **On the day I called, you answered me;**
> **you increased my strength of soul.**

The Lord, who is high, still regards the lowly,
but perceives the haughty from far away.
> **We shall sing of the ways of the Lord;**
> **for great is the glory of God!**

Though I walk in the midst of trouble, you save me.
You stretch out your hand, and your right hand delivers me.

> **Your steadfast love, O Lord, endures forever.**
> **Do not forsake me, but fulfill your purpose in me!**

Opening Prayer

God of bounty and abundance,
who calls forth blessings from the deep,
who bestows upon unworthy sinners both dignity and purpose:
we praise you for your holiness; we lift your name above everything;
we await your sending Word.

Call to Confession

To be in the presence of the holy God is to be aware of human sin.
As the prophet exclaimed, "Woe is me! For I am unclean!"
and as the apostle said, "I am a sinful man!"
so let us confess our sin in the presence of our holy God.

Prayer of Confession

Holy God,
you are all power and purity, truthfulness and love,
but we are a people of impure thoughts and profane speech,
of false and selfish motives.
We cannot stand in your presence,
unless in your patience you preserve us.
Touch us with your holy fire;
purify our thoughts, words, and actions;
call and send us with your gospel,
that all might be redeemed in Christ.

Declaration of Forgiveness

The Lord God of hosts is holy!
Indeed, God's glory fills the whole earth!
As you see the glory of God all around you,
be touched by the burning coal from God's altar.
Your guilt has departed, and your sin is blotted out.
Know that you are redeemed by the grace of Christ,
and live in peace.

Presentation of Tithes and Offerings

As Jesus shows us where to cast our nets, the catch belongs to the Lord.
As God has offered up wondrous blessings from the deep,
so may we offer to God that which is deepest within us and dearest to us.
In doing so, we ascribe to the Lord all grace and glory and goodness.

Prayer of Dedication

Great High God,
do not forsake the work of your own hands!
For we are your work, and we ask you to bring to fulfillment
the work you have begun in us.
Stretch out your hand and bless these offerings,
that the word you have given for our salvation,
and the work we do to glorify you, may never be in vain.

The Charge and Blessing

Give thanks to the Lord with your whole heart.
For the glory of the Lord fills the world around you.
Give your life of service to Jesus.
For the Christ who has purchased you calls you to follow.
Give body and soul as a temple to the Spirit.
For God's holiness will spare you from self-deception
and will give you your reason for being!

Sixth Sunday after Epiphany / Proper 1
Ordinary Time 6

Jeremiah 17:5–10

Psalm 1

1 Corinthians 15:12–20

Luke 6:17–26

In Preparation for Worship

Let me be like a tree
planted by streams of living water.
Fill me with your strength, that I may not be moved.
Ground me in your holy word,
that in your risenness,
I too might be raised
with all your church
and behold your blessed face.

Call to Worship

Let all who would be happy turn to the Lord.
For the Lord watches over the way of the righteous.
> **They are like trees planted by streams of water:**
> **healthy, fruitful, and prosperous.**

The wicked are like chaff in the wind.
They have turned their hearts away from the Lord.
> **Like a dry shrub in the desert,**
> **they do not see relief when it comes.**

Sixth Sunday after Epiphany / Proper 1— Ordinary Time 6 49

Do not be anxious, O people of God;
but take your delight in the law of the Lord!
> **We will meditate on it day and night;**
> **and the Lord will make us fruitful!**

Opening Prayer

Giver of Life, we thank you for the life we have in you,
and for the promise of new life we have in our resurrected Lord.
We praise you that the dead in Christ have not perished
and our faith in you is not in vain.

Call to Confession

Bring your cares, your troubles, your sins, and your woes.
Empty yourselves of all your burdens
and lay down all that weighs upon you.
Rest beside the still waters of the living Word,
meditate upon what God has taught you,
confess your need for grace and your desire for goodness,
and the Lord will surely heal you and make you prosper.

Prayer of Confession

Blessed God,
our only peace and consolation,
we seek your righteous answer to our poverty and wealth,
our fullness and hunger, our weeping and laughter.
We have enjoyed our times of blessedness
and endured our times of woe.
Through plenty and want, in joy and in sorrow,
we remain participants in this world of sin.
Forgive us, O God. Lift us out of our sin,
and justify us as members of Christ's risen body.

Declaration of Forgiveness

Jesus has promised to give laughter to the weeping, to fill the hungry with good things, to lift up the humble, to reward those who suffer in his name, and to welcome the poor into the ever new kingdom of God. In raising from the dead our Lord Jesus, who was unjustly executed for the sins of the world, God has begun the work of setting right all the injustices of the world through the great work of forgiveness. In Christ, this wonderful gift is offered to you. Accept it, and with it your new citizenship under the reign of God's peace.

Presentation of Tithes and Offerings

Those who live in and take their nourishment from God's holy word
have no cause for anxiety and nothing to fear.
Like trees that are steadily watered,
their leaves do not wither, but they yield good fruit in their season.
Let this season be the season of fullness and ripening.
Let us give of the fruits that we bear for the Lord.

Prayer of Dedication

Righteous God, you are ever giving to us, and so we give to you. You are ever blessing us, and so we bless you. May we never be too rich to be subjects of your kingdom. May we never be so full as to not know what it is like to be hungry. May we ever do all that we do in the name of Jesus, so that whether our neighbors bless or curse us, we might always be your own.

The Charge and Blessing

Let your roots grow deep into the very ground of God your Creator.
Seek the blessings of your Lord Jesus Christ.
Endure everything by the power of the Holy Spirit.
Bear good and lasting fruit for the eternal kingdom of God.

Seventh Sunday after Epiphany / Proper 2
Ordinary Time 7

Genesis 45:3–11, 15
Psalm 37:1–11, 39–40
1 Corinthians 15:35–38, 42–50
Luke 6:27–38

In Preparation for Worship

We wait upon you, O Lord,
in meekness, in trust, in delighted anticipation.
We would commit our ways unto you, O Lord,
knowing you will act.
We wait. We patiently wait.
As we wait, O God, inspire us with your goodness
to seek, to desire, and to do what is right.

Call to Worship

What is sown in dishonor is raised in glory.
    What is sown in weakness is raised in power.
What is sown a physical body is raised a spiritual body.
    We do not sow the body that is to be, but a bare seed.
God gives to each a body as God alone has chosen.
    Let us worship reverently;
    let us listen to and act boldly upon the word of our God,
    sowing generously the good news concerning Jesus Christ,
    that God may be glorified through our mortal bodies,
    and through the life that the Spirit gives us
    as the Body of Christ!

Opening Prayer

Creator God, you are the giver of life and of eternal life; you have fashioned our mortal bodies from the elements, our flesh and blood from the dust of the ground; yet you have destined us for an everlasting spiritual life in your imperishable kingdom. Therefore, we thank you that, though we entered this world bearing the image of our first ancestor, you have sent from heaven your Son, Jesus Christ, who grants us his imperishable and life-giving Spirit. Therefore, we gather to praise you, hoping to find rest in your presence, and to wait upon you, trusting that at the proper time, you will lead us into the chosen inheritance that, by your grace, we share with Christ.

Call to Confession

Truly the God who redeems can use even the hardness of the human heart to bring about glorious reconciliation. But such a redemption requires that hard hearts first be broken and contrite, humble and repentant, receptive to the love of Christ and to the double compassion that we see in him: the compassion of the Son for the Father, whose love has been spurned by the world, and the compassion of the Father for the Son, whose meek suffering and obedience to death for the sake of love is the final word on the sin of the world. Let us confess our sin to the One who has made such marvelous provision for our salvation.

Prayer of Confession

Loving and forgiving God, we confess that we have been selective with our love. We have favored those who favor us and ignored the unloved, the lonely, and the lost. We have been quick to judge, slow to bless, and slower still to give with absolute freedom, with no expectation of a return. Forgive us, O God, for all the ways in which we fall far short of perfection. Give us your Holy Spirit to inspire and sanctify us toward perfection in Christ, in whom alone we have every reason to hope and trust that we are indeed your children.

Declaration of Forgiveness

Do not be distressed, or angry with yourselves, for God's purpose in sending Christ Jesus is to preserve life, to preserve a faithful remnant on earth, who will worship the Lord; for truly, the salvation of the righteous is from the Lord; he is our refuge in the time of trouble. Commit your way to the Lord; trust in God, and he will make your vindication shine with the light of Christ, and the justice of your cause like the noonday sun. Know that in Christ Jesus you are forgiven and be at peace.

Presentation of Tithes and Offerings [Luke 6:34–38]

Jesus said, "If you lend to those from whom you hope to receive, what credit is that to you? Even sinners lend to sinners, to receive as much again. But love your enemies, do good, and lend, expecting nothing in return. Your reward will be great, and you will be children of the Most High; for he is kind even to the ungrateful and the wicked. Be merciful, just as your Father is merciful. Give, and it will be given to you. A good measure, pressed down, shaken together, running over, will be put into your lap; for the measure you give will be the measure you get back."

Prayer of Dedication

Eternal God, our life on earth soon fades and withers like grass; therefore we will envy no mortal, and we will ask for nothing in return for what we give. But we will content ourselves with the knowledge that you reward the meek and favor the humble, that they may delight in abundant prosperity. May these gifts be used in your Spirit so as to demonstrate your gospel of grace to the world and to reconcile those who are estranged from you and from your holy people. This we ask in Jesus' name.

The Charge and Blessing

Trust in the Lord, and do good;
so you will live in the land, and enjoy security.
Take delight in the Lord,
and he will give you the desires of your heart.

Eighth Sunday after Epiphany / Proper 3
Ordinary Time 8

Isaiah 55:10–13

Psalm 92:1–4, 12–15

1 Corinthians 15:51–58

Luke 6:39–49

In Preparation for Worship

The righteous flourish like the palm tree,
and grow like a cedar in Lebanon.
They are planted in the house of the Lord;
they flourish in the courts of our God.
In old age they still produce fruit;
they are always green and full of sap,
showing that the Lord is upright;
he is my rock, and there is no unrighteousness in him.

Call to Worship

It is good to give thanks to the Lord,
to sing praises to your name, O Most High;
> to declare your steadfast love in the morning,
> and your faithfulness by night,
to the music of the lute and the harp,
to the melody of the lyre.
> For you, O Lord, have made me glad by your work;
> at the works of your hands I sing for joy.

Opening Prayer

Truly, O God, you give us ample ground for rejoicing in your presence, a firm foundation on which to take our stand, build lives of faith in Christ, and give you praise. Establish us, we pray, in your wisdom and in your word, that we may weather the storms of life and bear the good fruit that testifies to hearts purified by your Spirit.

Call to Confession

Jesus warns us against hypocrisy, saying, "Why do you see the speck in your neighbor's eye, but do not notice the log in your own eye?" Only when we have rid our own eyes of their own large, blinding logs should we consider helping our neighbors with the minor specks that cloud their vision. Failing this, we risk personal ruin, like one who builds a house without a foundation, a house that will collapse at the first sign of adversity. Friends, let us confess the sins that blind us and the power of sin that binds us, the power from which we would have the Lord set us free.

Prayer of Confession

We confess, O Lord, that though we call you "Lord," we have not always done what you have commanded. We have blindly followed sightless guides who have lured us away from your reliable word. The wicked thoughts of our hearts have given rise to condemning judgments, cutting remarks, and cruel hypocrisy. Forgive us, we pray, O God, and change our hearts, that we may not offend you or cause others to stumble or fall away. Reform our ways in accordance with Christ Jesus, our Lord and Teacher, that we may be like him in every way and produce good fruit that is pleasing to you according to our nature as your reformed and obedient children.

Declaration of Forgiveness

The prophet declares, "You shall go out in joy, and be led back in peace," and he foretells a qualitative transformation: "Instead of the thorn shall come up the cypress; instead of the brier shall come up the myrtle; and it shall be to the Lord . . . an everlasting sign that shall not be cut off." And the apostle proclaims, "Listen, I will tell you a mystery! We will not all die, but we will all be changed, in a moment, in the twinkling of an eye, at the last trumpet. For the trumpet will sound, and the dead will be raised imperishable, and we will be changed." Therefore, I declare to you in the name of Christ Jesus: you are forgiven, free, and unfettered to live your life in faithful obedience and joyful peace. Thanks be to God, who gives us the victory through our Lord Jesus Christ!

Presentation of Tithes and Offerings

The Lord has resolved that the Word going forth from his mouth shall not return empty, but shall accomplish the divine and sovereign purpose, and succeed in the thing for which God has sent it into the world. Thus, the one in whom God is at work will produce good fruit and good treasure from the heart. Let us, therefore, offer the treasures and the produce of our life in the Lord.

Prayer of Dedication

Holy Lord, as you send the rain and the snow from heaven to water the earth, so you have provided your Word, to be sown as seed and to nourish as bread. We are truly blessed by your generous provision, and we long to share the joyful news of your goodness with those who are hungry, not only for temporal food, but for that which strengthens the heart and revives the spirit with the hope of eternal life. Receive and bless these gifts, we pray, that our labor may not be in vain, but that you might use them as seeds of salvation for the lost, the hungry, and the hopeless, those whom you are calling home to yourself, in Jesus' name.

The Charge and Blessing

Go and be fruitful, showing that the Lord is upright.
Be steadfast, immovable, always excelling in the work of the Lord,
for you know that in the Lord your labor is not in vain.

Last Sunday after Epiphany
(*Transfiguration Sunday*)

Exodus 34:29–35
Psalm 99
2 Corinthians 3:12–4:2
Luke 9:28–36 (37–43)

In Preparation for Worship

Where your Spirit is, O Lord, there is freedom;
where your image is revealed, your suffering love;
where your glory shines, your tender mercy.
We renounce the shameful things we have hidden.
We long for your Spirit and your freedom.
We desire to serve your holy truth.

Call to Worship

The Lord reigns! Let the peoples tremble! Let the earth quake!
> **Praise the awesome name of the Lord.**
> **For the Lord our God is holy!**

Mighty Sovereign, Lover of Justice,
you establish equity and righteousness among your people.
> **Extol the mighty name of the Lord.**
> **For the Lord our God is holy!**

God hears the people when they cry out.
The Lord has spoken from the pillar of cloud.
> **Worship at God's holy mountain.**
> **For the Lord our God is holy!**

Opening Prayer

God of Glory,
your light is eternal, yet hidden among us,
your Spirit is alive, yet veiled within us.
We praise you for your glory in our Lord Jesus Christ,
whose glory is seen in the suffering,
whose radiance is known at considerable cost,
whose image is recognized only when we turn to you.

Call to Confession

The glory of the law is a passing glory, for no one can obey it or fulfill it perfectly, no one but Christ Jesus, who has done so on our behalf. The glory of Christ is unsurpassed, unfading, permanent, and eternal. Therefore, let us turn to our God in the presence of Christ and confess our sin, our failure to keep the law, and our need for Christ's ministry of justification.

Prayer of Confession

Merciful God, you are forgiving of the humble, but avenging of the wrongdoings of the arrogant. Your glory that shines in the face of your servants and the glorified body of our suffering Lord make us bold to hope that you will heal us as we humbly seek your face. Lift the veil that covers our minds; soften our hardened hearts; transform us into reflections of your glory in Jesus Christ our Lord.

Declaration of Forgiveness

Only Jesus Christ, who has both fulfilled and set aside the law that would condemn us, gives us confidence toward God. Thus, let us henceforth renounce the shameful things that we keep hidden and refuse to practice cunning or to falsify God's word; but by the open statement of the truth let us commend ourselves to the conscience of everyone in the sight of God. By the Spirit of the living God, receive the grace of Jesus Christ and the competence we have in him to live a new life. For where the Spirit of the Lord is, there is freedom. Friends, believe the good news: the Spirit is here, and you are free.

Presentation of Tithes and Offerings

Since it is by God's mercy that we are engaged in this ministry,
we do not lose heart, but we have such a hope
that we may act with great boldness.
Let us, therefore, give with great boldness,
knowing that the Lord who is extolled with our gifts
can do mighty things with them as they are offered in faith.

Prayer of Dedication

Mighty Sovereign, Lover of Justice, Righteous God, Holy Lord,
you establish equity where there is injustice;
you speak clearly through clouds and confusion;
you have summoned us to listen to your chosen One,
your beloved Son, Jesus Christ.
Direct us now, we pray, in the use of these gifts,
which we humbly offer in the service of your glory.

The Blessing

Where the Spirit of the Lord is, there is freedom.
And all of us are being transformed into the image of Christ,
a transformation that comes from the Lord, the Spirit.
Therefore, go in the freedom of Christ,
seeing, rejoicing in, and testifying to the glory of God
wherever you go.

PART II

The Paschal Cycle
Lent—Easter—Pentecost

Ash Wednesday (ABC)

Joel 2:1–2, 12–17 OR Isaiah 58:1–12
Psalm 51:1–17
2 Corinthians 5:20b–6:10
Matthew 6:1–6, 16–21

IN PREPARATION FOR WORSHIP [see Joel 2:1–2, 12–17]
Holy God, your prophets speak of the day of the LORD
as a day of darkness and gloom, the great day of judgment;
and you desire a people set apart
from the corrupt and oppressive ways of the world.
Thus, we gather to express our sorrow,
to observe a somber season for rending our hearts,
and to return to you wholeheartedly,
knowing that you are gracious and merciful,
slow to anger and abounding in steadfast love.
As your prophets have summoned us, so we pray,
"Spare your people, O LORD,
and do not make your heritage a mockery,
a byword among the nations.
Why should it be said among the nations,
'Where is their God?'"

CALL TO WORSHIP [Psalm 51:15–17]
O LORD, open my lips,
> and my mouth will declare your praise.
For you have no delight in sacrifice or burnt offering.
> **But the sacrifice acceptable to God is a broken spirit;**
> **a broken and contrite heart, O God, you will not despise.**

or [Isaiah 58:9–12]

Remove the burdensome yoke from among you,
the pointing of the finger, the speaking of evil;
offer your food to the hungry
and satisfy the needs of the afflicted.
> **Then, surely, the light shall arise in the darkness**
> **and the gloom shall be dispersed, as at noon.**

The LORD shall guide you continually,
satisfy your needs in parched places,
and make your bones strong.
> **Make us, O LORD, like a well-watered garden,**
> **like a spring of water, whose waters never fail.**

Let your ancient ruins be rebuilt,
and the breach in your walls be repaired.
> **Establish, O LORD, new generations of the faithful.**
> **Come to us, and restore our streets for life**
> **in your gracious presence.**

OPENING PRAYER

Righteous and merciful God, your love is such that you desire our sanctification and you will not allow us to be content with hypocrisy or feigned piety. Though we know to seek you daily and make fitful efforts at unselfish deeds, we remain absorbed by self-interest. How soon we discover the limits of our compassion! But you continually call us to thoroughgoing repentance, complete obedience, and neighborly acts of mercy and love. Therefore, we seek you, O God, who alone can enable and inspire our obedience, who alone can restore us to useful service and sustain our willing discipleship and our service to those in need. Reveal yourself to us and speak your redeeming word, that we may embody the new creation you have in mind and serve as the ambassadors of Christ and his ministry of reconciliation; in Jesus' name.

LITANY OF PENITENCE [see Psalm 51]

Holy God, your judgments are just and beyond reproach;
we confess that we have sinned against you
and done what is evil in your sight.

Ash Wednesday (ABC)

Have mercy upon us, O God,
according to your steadfast love.
Holy God, you desire truth in the inward being
and love in outward deeds of mercy:
we confess we have not held fast to your truth
or shown compassion to the poor, the oppressed, and the suffering.
Have mercy upon us, O God,
according to your steadfast love.
Holy God, you call us to integrity,
but we have allowed self-concern to consume us,
and the needs of others to go unmet.
Have mercy upon us, O God,
according to your steadfast love.
According to your abundant mercy
blot out our transgressions.
Wash us thoroughly from all our iniquities,
and we shall be restored.
Forgive us, O God, and cleanse us from our sin.
Surely our transgressions are all known to you;
the very memory of them troubles us.
Forgive us, O God, and cleanse us from our sin.
Guilty from birth, we confess our hypocrisy.
Deluded by the flesh, we thirst for your wisdom.
Give us clean hearts, O God,
and restore to us the joy of your salvation.
Deliver us, O God, and we shall sing
and tell others of your deliverance!
Have mercy, O God, and be gracious to your penitent people.
Give us clean hearts, O God,
and restore to us the joy of your salvation,
for we pray in the name of Jesus Christ
our Redeemer and Lord.

Presentation of Tithes and Offerings
[Isaiah 58:5–9; Matthew 6:2–4]

Such a fast as the Lord envisions is deeply sabbatical: securing liberation
for the oppressed and sharing food, clothing, and shelter with the poor.

God's justice is not discursive; it is simply done without fanfare or partisan debate. Let us, therefore, do justice in accordance with the LORD's spirit of generous liberty. Let us offer our tithes, offerings, and alms to the LORD.

Prayer of Dedication

O Lord, on our own we have nothing, but in Christ we possess everything; before heaven we are poor, but in Christ we would make many rich. Receive and bless, therefore, these gifts, that they may, in your sight, be administered with grace, compassion, truthfulness, and integrity, and that the good news of your salvation, along with the simple gifts of basic provisions, might reach and give hope to those in need of help. We ask this for the praise of your glory and the vindication of your holy name.

The Blessing [see Matthew 6:19–21]

May your heart be forever fixed on the kingdom of God
and may you amass great treasure there, where no earthly thing—
neither thief nor moth, neither rust nor dust—can touch it,
but where all is secure in the watchful and merciful
presence of our Father in heaven.

First Sunday in Lent

Deuteronomy 26:1–11

Psalm 91:1–2, 9–16

Romans 10:8b–13

Luke 4:1–13

In Preparation for Worship

O Lord, you are my refuge and my fortress;
my God, in whom I trust.
Be my dwelling place, O Most High.
Guard me in all my ways, that no evil would befall your servant.
You, who in Christ Jesus suffered the scourge,
let the scourge afflict the members of your body no more.
Bear us up, O God, who are too weak to deliver ourselves.
Not to test you, but in simple trust,
we cast ourselves upon your mercy.

Call to Worship

If you confess that Jesus is Lord and believe in your heart
that God has raised him from the dead, then you will be saved.
> **Jesus is Lord! We confess it!**
> **We believe that God has raised him to new life!**
No one who believes in Christ Jesus will ever be put to shame.
> **The same Lord is Lord of all.**
> **God is generous to all who proclaim the word of faith.**
Everyone who calls upon the name of the Lord shall be saved.
> **We are gathered to call upon your holy name,**
> **O God of our salvation!**

Opening Prayer

O Lord Most High,
we seek to make our home in you,
to take shelter in your watchful presence.
Guard and protect us, saving God.
Answer us when we call to you.
Rescue in these evil times those who love you,
for we worship and serve you alone,
in Jesus' name.

Call to Confession

Though Jesus when tested was proven sinless, we ourselves make no such claim. Rather, it is with confidence in his righteousness that we confess our sins, for his perfection is our means of salvation. For he has said, "Those who love me, I will deliver; I will protect those who know my name. When they call to me, I will answer them; I will be with them in trouble, I will rescue them and honor them. With long life I will satisfy them, and show them my salvation." Let us confess our sins to God.

Prayer of Confession

**Holy God,
you have seen our troubles;
you have heard our thoughts;
you know our inward and outward pain.
Help us see where we have not been humble.
Guide us in confessing where we have been sinful.
Lead us through every time of testing and keep us from temptation,
that we may rely solely on you to prove us
in the faith we have been given
in Jesus Christ our Lord.**

Declaration of Forgiveness

The Lord has heard our voice and seen our affliction, our toil, and our oppression. The Lord has brought us out with a mighty hand and an outstretched arm, with a display of his power, and with signs and wonders. No one who believes in the Lord Jesus Christ will be put to shame. The Lord is generous to all who call on him. For everyone who calls on the name of the Lord shall be saved. Know and rest in the assurance that, in Jesus Christ, you are forgiven.

Presentation of Tithes and Offerings

God, who faithfully provides for all our needs and has given us in Christ Jesus an eternal inheritance, has instructed us to devote the first fruits of our labors in worship. Therefore, in thanksgiving, let us declare to the Lord our God that we trust in his promises, and let us place our gifts before our gracious God with rejoicing for all the bounty that God has given to us.

Prayer of Dedication

Ever-loving, ever-giving God, you have brought us into this place and given us innumerable provisions; as you led Israel into a land flowing with milk and honey, we too have enjoyed the blessings of your abundant creation. Therefore, we now bring you the produce of our lives that you, O Lord, have given us. Bless these gifts, we pray, with your consecrating Spirit, that their use might bring relief to the suffering, further your ministry, and give glory to your holy name.

The Charge and Blessing

The Word of God is near you, on your lips and in your heart:
Believers in the resurrection of Jesus Christ are justified.
Confessors of his Lordship are saved.
Therefore, go forth and proclaim this good news
for the sake of those who need to hear.

Second Sunday in Lent

Genesis 15:1–12, 17–18

Psalm 27

Philippians 3:17—4:1

Luke 13:31–35

In Preparation for Worship

Teach me your way, O Lord,
and I will inquire in your temple.
Shelter me in my day of trouble, and I will shout with joy.
Graciously hear me, and I will sing to you.
Lift me out of the depths, my Lord and my God,
and I shall lift up your name.

Call to Worship

Wait for the Lord.
Be strong, and let your heart take courage!
> **We will wait for the Lord.**
> **We shall see the goodness of God in the land of the living.**

Come, O people, and seek God's face!
> **Your face, O Lord, do we seek.**
> **Do not hide from us or turn away in anger.**

One thing I have asked of the Lord. That will I seek:
to live in the house of the Lord all the days of my life.
> **Behold the beauty of the Lord!**
> **God is my light and my salvation;**
> **of whom shall I be afraid?**

Opening Prayer

God of the Covenant,
who gives children to the barren and land to the homeless,
we praise you for your eternal faithfulness and your everlasting mercy.
Receive our songs of joy and our melodies of thanksgiving
as we send them up to your glorious heavens,
in Jesus' name.

Call to Confession

The Lord is our shield and our shelter! Jesus, when he came casting out demons and performing miracles of healing, expressed his longing to gather Jersualem as a hen gathers her chicks; though his first listeners were not willing to be so gathered, ultimately, he gathered many, drawing not only Jersualem but a world of sinners of every age, under his outstretched arms on the cross. Friends, setting aside all resistance, let us be gathered to God in confession, through the ministry of Jesus Christ.

Prayer of Confession

God of Heaven, we confess that we often fear defeat and fail to trust you, for we both overestimate and underestimate the enemies of the cross of Christ. We have forgotten heavenly things and set our minds on earthly things. We have gloried in shameful acts, dismissed your word as spoken through the prophets, and ignored the holy deeds you have commanded us to do. Save us and forgive us, O God. Transform the body of our humiliation that it may be conformed to the body of your glory in Jesus Christ our Lord.

Declaration of Forgiveness

Blessed is the one who comes in the name of the Lord! Blessed is the sovereign power of God. Truly, by faith in God and his covenant, our citizenship is in heaven, and it is from there that we are expecting the return of our Savior, the Lord Jesus Christ. Friends, believe the promises of God. Even if those who are dearest to you were to forsake you, the Lord would take you up. He will not cast you off, for the Lord is our stronghold and our salvation. In Jesus Christ we are forgiven. Therefore, let us rejoice in the Lord!

Presentation of Tithes and Offerings

As the psalmist has sung, I believe that I shall see the goodness of the Lord in the land of the living! I will offer in his tent sacrifices with shouts of joy! With such faith, hope, and joy, let us render unto God our tithes and our offerings of thanks.

Prayer of Dedication

Hear, O Lord, as we cry aloud; be gracious and give answer!
For we, your people, would render you praise for your provision,
gratitude for your kindness, and faith in response to your faithfulness.
Bless these gifts, we pray, that they, and we, may testify to the world
that you are good to those who trust in you;
this we ask in Jesus' name.

The Charge and Blessing

Look toward heaven and count the stars, if you are able.
So shall be those who come to saving faith in the Son of God.
So shall be those made righteous in Jesus Christ.
Go, therefore, in faith and without fear,
confident that the Lord, the triune God, leads you on a level path.

Third Sunday in Lent

Isaiah 55:1–9
Psalm 63:1–8
1 Corinthians 10:1–13
Luke 13:1–9

In Preparation for Worship

From the ways through the lowlands of our thoughts,
we seek passage to your highlands, O God.
From the wretched ways we have carved upon the earth,
we seek the path to your kingdom of heaven.
Grant us passage. Show us your way.

Call to Worship

O God, you are my God. I seek you. My soul thirsts for you!
My flesh faints for you, as in a dry and weary land.
> **I look for you in the sanctuary, O God,**
> **to behold your power and glory.**

Your steadfast love, O God, is better than life itself.
> **So I will bless you as long as I live.**
> **I will raise my hands and call upon your name.**

When I think of you on my bed, and meditate on you in the night,
I am satisfied and filled with praises, for you have been my help.
> **In the shadow of God's wings, I will sing for joy.**
> **I will cling to the Lord, who upholds me.**

Opening Prayer

O God our Provider, who pours out living water from Christ our spiritual rock, who gives us food from Christ our living bread, who provides us with a way out of trouble through Christ our way, help us endure in faith through this season of testing and strengthen us with your word, that we may stand in your holy presence.

Call to Confession

Come. Let us surrender to God all that is dead in our lives, trusting in the Lord's patience and care to stimulate new growth, trusting also in God's judgment that fruitfulness is necessary for life, even as waste is fatal. Let us forsake every wicked, wasteful way and disown every ugly, unrighteous thought. Let us return to the Lord our God, who grants pardon in abundance and freely offers the water of life to satisfy our parched and withering souls.

Prayer of Confession

God of Mercy,
we surrender the fruitlessness of our strivings;
we confess our need for your care;
we admit we are quick to lose hope,
to squander our substance on that which does not satisfy,
to distrust what we cannot buy.
Have mercy on us, O God, as we turn to you.
Help us trust in your grace.

Declaration of Forgiveness

Although everyone is tested, God is faithful, who does not allow us to be tested beyond our strength but provides the way out so that we may be able to endure it. Our supreme consolation and provision from God is Jesus Christ, who intercedes for us and abundantly pardons all those who return to the Lord. He is a witness to all peoples and heir of God's everlasting covenant with David. Be assured, therefore, that in Jesus Christ, you who seek the Lord are forgiven and have peace with God.

Presentation of Tithes and Offerings

Surely the Lord satisfies our faint, weary, and hungry flesh with spiritual food and spiritual drink, placing a limit on human suffering, but giving us countless reasons to praise him with joy and thanksgiving. Therefore, let us make our heartfelt offerings in praise of our triune God.

Prayer of Dedication

O God, we have beheld your power and glory.
Truly, your steadfast love is better than life,
therefore, we will bless you all our lives long.
You who have been our help and have satisfied our needs,
receive and bless these offerings,
that they may be used in your name
to help those in need
and to testify to the truth that your grace
is freely given in love,
through Jesus Christ our Lord.

The Charge and Blessing

Seek the Lord while he may be found,
call upon him while he is near.
Partake of the Spirit's generous presence and free provision,
and may God's holy words and righteous ways
be revealed to the world, wherever you go,
in the name of Jesus Christ.

Fourth Sunday in Lent

Joshua 5:9–12

Psalm 32

2 Corinthians 5:16–21

Luke 15:1–3, 11b–32

In Preparation for Worship

While I kept silence, my body wasted away
through my groaning all day long.
Day and night your hand was heavy upon me;
my strength was dried up as by the heat of summer.
But like the prodigal son who, having squandered everything,
came to himself, I said, "I will get up and go to my father . . ."

Call to Worship

Let all who are faithful offer prayer to you, O God;
> at a time of distress, the rush of mighty waters
> shall not reach them.

You, O Lord, are a hiding place for me;
> you preserve me from trouble;
> you surround me with glad cries of deliverance.

"I will instruct you and teach you the way you should go;
I will counsel you with my eye upon you."
Many are the torments of the wicked,
> but steadfast love surrounds those who trust in the Lord.

Be glad in the Lord and rejoice, O righteous,
> and shout for joy, all you upright in heart!

Opening Prayer

Eternal God, you are gracious and compassionate, quick to welcome your children into your presence, ready to rejoice when we come to recognize and honor your generous, loving, and forgiving nature. Receive us, we pray, and look upon us with favor as we gather to worship you, to offer you our loyalty, and to render our joyful thanksgiving for the kindness you have shown us—kindness far beyond what our thoughts and deeds deserve.

Call to Confession

Happy are those whose transgression is forgiven, whose sin is covered. Happy are those to whom the Lord imputes no iniquity, and in whose spirit there is no deceit. Friends, let us not hide our iniquity, but let us acknowledge our sin to God; for when we confess our transgressions to the Lord, God is gracious to forgive the guilt of our sin.

Prayer of Confession

Holy God, merciful and forgiving, who in Jesus Christ welcomes sinners and eats with them, we confess that we have often acted stubbornly, going our own way; we have often shown an ill temper and how little we understand your ways; we have used your resources to indulge ourselves, and failed to conduct ourselves as befits members of your royal family. We have sinned against heaven and before you. Forgive us, we pray, and roll away the disgrace of our past sins, in Jesus' name.

Declaration of Forgiveness

Hear the good news: in Christ God was reconciling the world to himself, not counting our trespasses against us, but for our sake he made him to be sin who knew no sin, so that in Christ we might become the righteousness of God. All this is from God, who reconciled us to himself through Christ, and has given us the ministry of reconciliation. So if anyone is in Christ, there is a new creation: everything old has passed away; see, everything has become new!

Presentation of Tithes and Offerings

Our loving God, who celebrates the homecoming of repentant sinners with a lavish feast, has entrusted the good news of reconciliation to us. To his faithful children God says, "All that is mine is yours." Therefore, let us, as Christ's ambassadors, devote our gifts for the furtherance of Christ's mission, trusting wholeheartedly in God to make them effective, so that through us God might indeed appeal to those who are lost or have wandered far from home.

Prayer of Dedication

Gracious God,
you are generous beyond our comprehension,
giving of your own Son that we might be made righteous,
and honoring sinners who return home.
In gratitude for your merciful ways toward us,
we offer you these gifts in celebration of your goodness,
that as you inspire us to use them well,
we might see new life emerge among us,
and the lost returning home, in Jesus' name.

The Charge and Blessing

Friends in Christ, from now on
let us regard no one from a human point of view;
but let us regard each one from God's point of view,
who loves and desires reconciliation with the whole world.
Go, therefore, entreating others on behalf of Christ
to be reconciled to God,
and may the Holy Spirit bless you with joy and peace
as you serve as ambassadors of the triune God.

Fifth Sunday in Lent

Isaiah 43:16–21

Psalm 126

Philippians 3:4b–14

John 12:1–8

In Preparation for Worship

Call me upward, O God.
Enable me to share, like Jesus Christ, my Lord,
in the sufferings of your people.
Let me know the power of your Spirit
by the resurrection and renewal of this body.

Call to Worship

Do not remember the former things,
or consider the things of old.
> **For the Lord is about to do a new thing!**

Now it springs forth.
Do you not perceive it?
> **The Lord has prepared a way in the wilderness,**
> **and rivers in the desert to give us drink.**

Declare God's praise, O people!
Honor the Lord, with every living thing!
> **We thank you, mighty God!**
> **We declare your praise!**

Opening Prayer

O Lord, you have done great things for us in the past; be with us in this present time and restore our fortunes in Christ, that the seeds we have sown in tears and the losses we have endured may bear for you a harvest of joy.

Call to Confession

Whatever righteousness is yours due to observing the law,
whatever gains you have made through good deeds,
know they are nothing apart from personal knowledge of Jesus Christ.
So relinquish every former, fruitless way,
all sin and every reason for self-justification,
and receive the righteousness that is yours
in covenant with Christ Jesus our Lord.

Prayer of Confession

**O Lord our God,
you have done great things for us;
you have graciously chosen and formed your people
that we might worship you and declare your praise.
Yet, we confess, we often forget our joyful calling;
we foolishly place confidence in the flesh,
as though we had reason to boast or a righteousness of our own.
Forgive us, O God, for every failure of our faith and worship,
for every forgetful moment when we lose sight of Christ,
who alone is righteous and mighty to save.
Restore us, we pray, and exchange joy for our tears,
faith for our sin, righteousness for our self-regard;
this we ask in Jesus' name.**

Declaration of Forgiveness

In Christ alone we stand to gain that which is worth more than everything! The past is gone, is counted as loss, and you are forgiven in Christ! Now press on toward the goal, not because it already belongs to you, but because you now belong to Jesus Christ. Forget the past, and strain forward to what lies ahead. Press on toward the prize of the upward call of God in Christ Jesus our Lord!

Presentation of Tithes and Offerings

Jesus said, "You always have the poor with you, but you do not always have me." Thus, the care of the poor is indeed the continual concern of the church, as is our calling to honor the presence of the Lord. Neither is optional, both are needful. One concerns mission, the other worship. Therefore, let us offer our gifts for the worship of God in Christ and for the care of those in need.

Prayer of Dedication

Holy God, truly there is no greater gain than to know Christ Jesus our Lord. Though we suffer the loss of all things, yet in Christ they are restored, for the gospel he has given us as seed for sowing shall produce a great harvest of joy. Bless, therefore, these gifts, we pray, that they may indeed be used in keeping with your will, for the comfort of the poor, for the redemption of the lost, and for the joyful praise of our risen Redeemer.

The Charge and Blessing

Friends, God is doing a new thing.
Christ Jesus has made you his own!
Therefore, forgetting what lies behind
and straining forward to what lies ahead,
press on toward the goal for the prize
of the heavenly call of God in Christ Jesus.
And may the blessing of the triune God,
who restores all things, be upon you.

Sixth Sunday in Lent (*Palm Sunday*)

Isaiah 50:4–9a
Psalm 118:1–2, 19–29
Philippians 2:5–11
Luke 19:28–40

IN PREPARATION FOR WORSHIP

Morning by morning you awaken me, O Lord;
you awaken my ear to listen.
Morning by morning, you sustain me with your word,
weary though I am.
Open my ear once again, O Lord,
that I may listen as one who is taught.
For you, O God, are the one true teacher,
and I shall not presume to teach others
unless I am taught by your Son and your Servant,
Jesus Christ, who lives and reigns with you and the Holy Spirit,
one God, both now and forever.

CALL TO WORSHIP

This is the day that the Lord has made;
> **let us rejoice and be glad in it.**

O give thanks to the Lord, for he is good;
> **his steadfast love endures forever!**

Let Israel say,
> **"His steadfast love endures forever."**

Open to me the gates of righteousness,
that I may enter through them
and give thanks to the Lord.
> This is the gate of the Lord;
> the righteous shall enter through it.

Opening Prayer

Almighty God, your powerful deeds are praiseworthy, for you shed light upon your searching, hopeful people and you inspire even the stones to shout of your glory! We come in festal procession to the horns of your altar, offering you, our sovereign God, the song of praise that echoes down the ages and fills your courts on high: "Blessed is the king who comes in the name of the Lord! Peace in heaven, and glory in the highest heaven!"

Call to Confession

Christ Jesus did not exploit his equality with God, but emptied and humbled himself, and became obedient even to the point of death on a cross. Though God, he was born a human; though holy, he became a slave, that we who are sinners might be raised up and set free from the power of sin. Therefore, let us not think of ourselves too highly, but let us have the same mind that was in Christ Jesus. Let us humbly confess our sin and our need for this great intervention that Jesus has performed for our salvation.

Prayer of Confession

Our Father in heaven, your Son was not rebellious when destined for the cross, but surrendered himself to those who insulted, mocked, struck, tortured, and killed him. For all this, he was not disgraced or put to shame, for you have vindicated and exalted him who suffered all for our salvation. We confess, O God, we are unworthy, for we have been rebellious, not obedient; we have sought comfort rather than suffer willingly for your name's sake. Save us, we beseech you, O Lord, for the sake of Jesus' great intercession. Forgive us our sins and establish our faith on Christ our cornerstone. May the name of our Savior and Lord, Jesus Christ, be exalted above all, for your divine glory.

Declaration of Forgiveness

Who will contend with those for whom Christ died?
It is the Lord God who helps us; who will declare us guilty?
All accusers will wear out like a garment;
the moth will eat them up.
Our salvation is the Lord's doing;
it is marvelous in our eyes.
Therefore, let every knee bend at the name of Jesus,
and let every tongue confess that Jesus Christ is Lord,
to the glory of God the Father.

Presentation of Tithes and Offerings

God is sovereign over all things! Yet even the Son of God was not above borrowing a colt for his procession into Jerusalem, instructing his disciples to tell the owners, "The Lord needs it"; and it was promptly sent to serve him. Likewise, when told to silence his worshipping disciples, Jesus declared, "If these were silent, the stones would shout out." Therefore, let nothing oppose or obstruct the redemptive mission of Christ in the world, and let nothing detract from the glory that is due him. Let us devote our gifts to the service of God.

Prayer of Dedication

O God, you are our God;
we give you thanks and extol you,
for you are exceedingly good,
and your steadfast love endures forever.
Bless these gifts by your redeeming grace,
that our stewardship may serve to draw others
into the fellowship of those who know Jesus as Lord,
who bend the knee to him and confess his name,
the name that is above all other names,
the name in which we pray.

The Charge and Blessing

Blessed is the one who comes in the name of the Lord.
And blessed are you as you go forth from the house of the Lord,
bearing the good news of the grace of God in Jesus Christ,
and the promised Holy Spirit to inspire your ongoing worship and witness.

Sixth Sunday in Lent (*Passion Sunday*)

Isaiah 50:4-9a

Psalm 31:9-16

Philippians 2:5-11

Luke 22:14-23:56 OR Luke 23:1-49

IN PREPARATION FOR WORSHIP

Surrounded by the deep darkness of this generation,
we turn our thoughts to you, O heavenly Father.
We are mindful of the mission of your Son, Jesus Christ;
therefore, awaken us, make us watchful,
and keep us from the time of trial.
Yes, keep us from the time of trial, and make us ever grateful
that Jesus has fulfilled the Scriptures
and undergone the great trial on our behalf.

CALL TO WORSHIP

Be gracious to me, O LORD, for I am in distress;
my eye wastes away from grief, my soul and body also.
> For my life is spent with sorrow, and my years with sighing;
> my strength fails because of my misery, and my bones waste away.

I am the scorn of all my adversaries, a horror to my neighbors,
an object of dread to my acquaintances;
those who see me in the street flee from me.
> I have passed out of mind like one who is dead;
> I have become like a broken vessel.

For I hear the whispering of many— terror all around!—
as they scheme together against me, as they plot to take my life.

> But I trust in you, O Lord;
> I say, "You are my God."

My times are in your hand;
deliver me from the hand of my enemies and persecutors.
> Let your face shine upon your servant;
> save me in your steadfast love.

Opening Prayer

Almighty and merciful God, you alone are worthy to be called Lord, for yours is the authority above which there is no other. Yet your Son, the Lord Jesus Christ, has come to us as one who serves. Surrendering his body to death and commiting his spirit into your hands, Jesus endured sorrow and suffering, interceded for sinners, and showed himself steadfast and obedient to the end. As we gather to remember his great misery and passion, send your Spirit to us to direct our hearts to worship you aright, to remind us of all that caused the sun's light to fail and the veil to be torn, and to give us faith that our remembrance is no reenactment, but a new act of worship in the presence of the risen and ascended Christ, whose death was once for all, and whose life is forever and inextinguishable.

Call to Confession

Jesus warned his disciples that, despite their best intentions, the accuser wants to sift us like wheat; yet Jesus also promised Peter, who denied knowing Jesus in his hour of need, that he himself would pray for his disciple, that his faith would not fail. In keeping with the will of Jesus our intercessor, let us turn again to our Savior and confess our sins, knowing that he alone who was innocent of transgressions, and declared innocent by both Pilate who sentenced him and the very centurion who oversaw his execution, is able to deliver us from the power of sin.

Prayer of Confession

Holy God, what forces of darkness conspired to take the life of your Son, and what obedience he showed, what anguish he endured, in accepting your will that he should suffer death for us! Forgive us, O God, for our sinful state, that such a sacrifice was ever needful. Forgive us for slumbering through circumstances that grieve you to the heart. Forgive us for grieving for the wrong things, for failing to recognize the righteous,

the faithful, and the humble among us. Strengthen us, we pray, for Christlike obedience, that we may have the mind of Christ to instruct us, the name of Christ to empower us, and the love of Christ to inspire us to glorify you in loyalty and to serve you with patient endurance.

Declaration of Forgiveness

Such is the grace of Jesus Christ that, even as our Savior was being crucified, he interceded for those who put him to death, saying, "Father, forgive them; for they do not know what they are doing." Ignoring the baiting taunts of onlookers that he should save himself, he promised a thief who was dying alongside him, one who acknowledged and believed that Jesus was indeed about to inherit his kingdom, "Truly I tell you, today you will be with me in Paradise." Friends, in light of the majesty, mercy, forgiveness, and grace that we see in Jesus' obedience, even in the face of death, rest assured that you are most certainly forgiven in his name.

Presentation of Tithes and Offerings

As Jesus conferred on his disciples a kingdom, so he calls us to exercise good judgment in our adminstration of his provisions. As the disciples lacked nothing while they accompanied Jesus in his earthly ministry, so we lack nothing needful as we minister in his living presence. Let us entrust our gifts and our offerings to God, dedicating them to the sovereign ministry of Christ.

Prayer of Dedication

Sovereign God,
whose beloved Son, Jesus Christ,
is seated at the right hand of your power:
our gifts cannot compare with the great outpouring of love
that led Jesus to take up the cross and to die upon it,
laden with the sin of the world.
Teach us to give with such humility,
with such mindfulness of your will,
with such depth of trust in you
that these gifts and our very lives might reflect
your glory as we have witnessed it in Jesus,

whose name is exalted above every name,
and whose praises we sing, with all your creation,
in adoration and thanksgiving.

The Charge and Blessing

Be of one mind, that of Christ Jesus.
Go in humility, in the power of Christ's name.
Seek the will of God in everything,
and let your life be an offering
in the service of the Holy Spirit.

Monday of Holy Week (ABC)

Isaiah 42:1–9

Psalm 36:5–11

Hebrews 9:11–15

John 12:1–11

In Preparation for Worship

You have called us, O Lord, in righteousness,
in the name of Christ Jesus in whom you delight.
As you sent him in mercy, to bring forth justice,
so let your Spirit lead and enlighten us,
that we might declare your grace to the nations
and spread his teaching abroad.

Call to Worship

God alone is glorious, who made the heavens and the earth.
The Lord is his name, whose steadfast love surpasses all.
> **Your judgments are deep, your faithfulness high,**
> **your mercy wide, your tenderness sure.**

Come, take refuge in the shadow of his wings,
for the feast is prepared and the sanctuary is open.
> **Those in bondage, in darkness and sin,**
> **those who hunger and thirst are welcome.**

In the name of Christ, God's chosen one,
come eat and drink from his gracious abundance.
> **Let us taste your love and salvation, O Lord!**
> **Let us bask in your light and know purity of heart!**

Opening Prayer

Gracious God, your grace and mercy reaches to the heavens and abounds to the farthest corners of the earth. All may take refuge and find nurture in you! Where people languish and are lost in darkness, you search them out with the light of your Word and you send your Spirit to call them home. In your anointed, you have redeemed the broken, healed the sick, and established justice in the earth, that your kingdom may be seen and celebrated and anticipated in its fullness. Come, therefore, and uphold your servant people, gathered for worship, that we, though humble, may offer glory to you and to no other, in Jesus' name.

Call to Confession

A death has occurred that redeems us, an offering that far exceeds all the ancient rites of purification. Christ has entered the Holy Place for us, to obtain that which we could never secure for ourselves, to liberate us from the futility of sin and death. Let confess our sins and our deep need of this gracious gift by which we are redeemed and set free for life, love, and service.

Prayer of Confession

Living God, you have called us to holiness, but we have defiled the flesh; you have called us to faithfulness, but we have transgressed your covenant. Therefore, your Son Jesus Christ has interceded for us, once for all, offering you pure worship with his own blood and obtaining for us a promised inheritance, eternal redemption, and innumerable good things to come. Establish us anew in Christ, we pray; anoint us afresh with him, that our sins may be buried and that we, unworthy though we are, may be restored, emerge unblemished, and be filled with your eternal Spirit, to live with and worship you as we ought; in Jesus' name we pray.

Declaration of Forgiveness

Whatever cleansing was once promised by the sacrificial system of old has been altogether surpassed and superseded by the blood of Christ, who in the grace of the Holy Spirit offered himself for our sakes. Without sin, stain, or blemish, Jesus Christ the Son of God is the mediator of a new covenant, according to which your conscience is now free from guilt and from bondage to dead works in order that you might now live for God and offer your lives in service, devotion, thanksgiving, and adoration. Know therefore that in Jesus Christ you are forgiven and be at peace.

Presentation of Tithes and Offerings

Jesus said the poor would always be with the church, and truly the church should never be without, above, or forgetful of its mission to serve those in need. But neither should we hold anything back from serving the Lord, caring for his body, and offering the best we have, so that the fragrance of Christ might fill the church and the world. Let us offer our gifts, for the blessing of the church and for the continuance of Christ's mission, to our loving, self-giving Savior.

Prayer of Dedication

Lord, preserve your church, poor though we are before the majesty of heaven, small though we are amidst your vast creation. Build up your church, we pray, by guiding us and directing these your gifts to the ministries and missions and acts of service to which you would lead us. Nurture your church on the true bread of mission, on the works of love and compassion that you have prepared for us to do, that all who witness and receive from your church in the world, be they poor in any way, might know that you are with them, and that you have come to call them to yourself and illumine the way home.

The Blessing

Drink and delight in the river of life.
Walk in the light that bathes you with light.
Follow the Christ who has gone before you
and who calls you now to the way of the cross.

Tuesday of Holy Week (ABC)

Isaiah 49:1–7
Psalm 71:1–14
1 Corinthians 1:18–31
John 12:20–36

IN PREPARATION FOR WORSHIP

O LORD, who formed your servant in the womb
to glorify you and to reflect the light of your life and wisdom:
as we remember the great labor of your Son Jesus Christ,
give us your strength; teach us your wisdom;
let your church show forth your glory,
that those whom you call might be gathered to you,
and that our labors for the gospel might not be in vain.

CALL TO WORSHIP [Isaiah 49:7; Psalm 71:3]

Thus says the LORD, the Redeemer of Israel and his Holy One,
to one deeply despised, abhorred by the nations, the slave of rulers:
> Kings shall see and stand up, princes,
> and they shall prostrate themselves.
Because the LORD is faithful;
the Holy One of Israel has chosen you.
> You are a rock of refuge, O LORD,
> a strong and mighty fortress to save!

OPENING PRAYER

Holy God, we gather in the name of Jesus Christ, for you have drawn us into your presence. We gather, and would glorify your name, for the light that we have seen in your Son, for the truth we have heard in his Word, for the Spirit that is the very source of our life. We gather to hear anew and be reminded of your wisdom which, though despised by the world, is nevertheless that which we believe for the gift of salvation. Speak to us, O God, in this hour, whether in the voice of thunder or in the deep stillness of our hearts; but speak, that we may see Jesus lifted up in our midst.

CALL TO CONFESSION [John 12:24–26a]

Jesus said, "Very truly, I tell you, unless a grain of wheat falls into the earth and dies, it remains just a single grain; but if it dies, it bears much fruit." Thus, Jesus spoke of his sacrificial death; but in so doing, he also called his disciples to follow him and participate in his pattern of self-surrender: "Whoever serves me must follow me, and where I am, there will my servant be also." Trusting, therefore, in the one who leads us to repentance by summoning us to die to sin, let us confess our sins together.

PRAYER OF CONFESSION

Almighty God, you call us to walk in the light of Christ, but we confess the darkness of the world has often deceived and seduced us; though you would have us be children of light, a light to the nations, we have failed to faithfully present Christ to the world, for our light has grown dim and our zeal has failed. Forgive us, O LORD. Incline your ear and save your people, for in you we seek refuge. In your righteousness, deliver and forgive us; in your judgment, drive out the ruler of this world from among your people. Let the wisdom of your light shine among us again. Let the presence of Christ be known among us, that you might draw all to yourself, in Jesus' name.

DECLARATION OF FORGIVENESS
[1 Corinthians 1:18, 30; Psalm 71:14]

Those who are perishing regard the cross as foolishness, but to us who are being saved it is the power of God. Indeed, Jesus Christ the crucified has become for us our sanctification and redemption. Therefore, since we have been forgiven and redeemed in Christ, let us hope in God continually and praise the Lord evermore.

Presentation of Tithes and Offerings

In life and in mission, God chooses what is foolish in the world to shame the wise; what is weak in the world to shame the strong; things that are low and despised to reduce to nothing those things that are held in honor by the world. If God can do so with humble people, how much more might the Lord use our simple offerings with glorious results? Let us dedicate our gifts, be they large or small, to the service of God.

Prayer of Dedication

Surely, O Lord, our cause is with you, whose seeming foolishness far surpasses human understanding, whose weakness puts all human strength to shame. No one can boast in your presence, O God, except to boast about you and all that you have done in Christ to bring about your righteousness and the light that gives us life. Bless, therefore, these humble offerings, that they too may be used for your glory, in the name of Jesus Christ our Lord.

The Blessing

Let your mouth be filled with the praise of the Lord.
Let your tongue tell of his glory all day long.
Lift up the name of Jesus, wherever you go,
that those nearby and known to you
and those afar off in distant lands
might hear the gospel of Christ's saving grace
and that salvation might reach to the ends of the earth.

Wednesday of Holy Week (ABC)

Isaiah 50:4–9a
Psalm 70
Hebrews 12:1–3
John 13:21–32

In Preparation for Worship

Awaken us, O Lord; awaken us and speak.
Speak that faith may arise in our hearts
and issue in such obedience as we see in Jesus Christ,
the Pioneer of our faith, the teacher of wisdom
who sustains the weary with your Word.

Call to Worship

Seek the Lord!
Rejoice and be glad!
> **God is great! We declare it continually.**
> **The salvation of the Lord is sure.**

Look to Jesus, whose faith is perfect,
who did not waver in the face of suffering.
> **Christ is Lord, our help and our deliverer,**
> **our pioneer, our teacher, our redeemer.**

Speak, O Lord, with your awakening Spirit.
Sustain and revive us with your powerful word.
> **Morning by morning the Lord greets and instructs us.**
> **Let us give fresh attention to the Word of the Lord.**

Opening Prayer

Holy God, what faithfulness we see in your servant, your Son Jesus Christ, who did not turn back from the betrayal, the insults, and the suffering that he knew awaited him. What perseverance, what obedience, what faith, what glory! For where he is rejected, his glory is ensured by the departure of evil from his presence, and where he is received his glory is enhanced as those who love your salvation praise his name! Either way, your Son is glorified in all that he endured for the joy that was set before him. Come, O God, Father, Son, and Holy Spirit, that we may exult in your righteous presence and be taught by the word that you would speak to us today.

Call to Confession [Hebrews 12:1–3]

Consider all the hostility Jesus endured from sinners for the sake of the joy set before him, and do not grow weary or lose heart. But instead, let us trust him who suffered the humiliation of the cross for our sake, and confess our sin, that we, free and unburdened, might faithfully persevere in following Christ, who through his perfect obedience has brought faith to perfection.

Prayer of Confession

Divine Deliverer, you have promised your salvation to those who seek you. We confess, however, that we have not listened or sought your will as we should; we have rebelled and gone our own way; we have been quick to find fault with others, yet failed to offer you the obedience of true faith. Forgive us, O God, and hasten to help us. Awaken us to listen; set us free from every spirit of deception; put us back on the straight and narrow course that leads to you, for truly you are great and your salvation is our best and only hope; in Jesus' name we pray.

Declaration of Forgiveness
[Hebrews 12:1–3; Isaiah 50:7–9; Psalm 70:4–5]

Jesus, the pioneer of faith, is seated at the right hand of power; yet he who died for our vindication is near; we have not been disgraced. What the world regarded as a shameful death, he has endured for our help and salvation. If Christ then, who is enthroned on high, is your refuge and deliverer, who is there to declare you guilty? No, your accusers are consumed; they are worn out like rags. Therefore, rejoice and be glad and say evermore: the Lord is great, for Christ has become our salvation. Thanks be to God.

Presentation of Tithes and Offerings

We follow Jesus Christ and a great cloud of witnesses who have testified to God's glory and persevered in covenant loyalty, leaving us a heritage of faith and inspiring us with the hope of joy. Let us therefore offer our gifts in accordance with this legacy, mindful of the witness that we ourselves shall leave for the encouragement of coming generations.

Prayer of Dedication

O Lord our God, you are immortal and eternal, yet in Jesus Christ you endured suffering and death for the sake of all humanity. We are but poor and needy, knowing that no temporal or earthly provision can purchase the great salvation that Christ alone has secured on our behalf. Therefore, O God, receive these offerings of gratitude and thanksgiving, that they might serve as our testimony to your faithful and all-sufficient provision in Jesus Christ, your obedient Son and our beloved Savior, in whose name we pray.

The Blessing

Set your heart on the salvation of Christ
and say evermore, "God is great!"
Follow the Lord Jesus with perseverance and faith,
mindful of the witness that you add to the chorus.
And may the Holy Spirit of hope and joy
keep you awake and attuned to the Word:
your pioneer, your teacher, your reward.

Maundy Thursday (ABC)

Exodus 12:1–4 (5–10) 11–14

Psalm 116:1–2, 12–19

1 Corinthians 11:23–26

John 13:1–17, 31b–35

IN PREPARATION FOR WORSHIP

We would enter your courts, O Lord,
and lift up the cup of salvation.
We would draw near and partake of your presence,
remember your death, and anticipate your return.
Therefore, we pray, prepare us, O God,
with gratitude for how you have spared us,
with loyalty for how you have served us,
with hope in all you have promised,
and with the love that itself proclaims to the world
that we belong to you.

CALL TO WORSHIP
[Exodus 12:14; Psalm 116:17; 1 Corinthians 11:25]

Let this day be a day of remembrance.
Celebrate it as a festival to the LORD.
> **For by the sign of the blood of the lamb**
> **the LORD spared Israel of old.**
And by the body and blood of Christ
we partake of the new covenant.
> **Let us remember and give thanks**
> **and call on the name of the LORD.**

Opening Prayer [John 13:1, 3]

O God our Father, you have given all things into the hands of your Son Jesus Christ, whom you sent to reveal your gracious and loving nature to this world. Thus, Christ our Lord and teacher withheld nothing but gave up everything. Having loved his own who were in the world, he loved them to the end, and he gave his disciples an example of love that we too are to follow, a new commandment that we too are to obey. We thank you, O God, for your example of love, your command to love, and for your unending deeds of love; and we thank you that the love of Christ has made its way down to us, in our generation, that we, assured of your love, may live as servants of your love in the midst of this generation.

Call to Confession

The LORD is just and will execute judgment on sin, but those who are marked with the blood of the Lamb of God he will pass over and no plague shall touch them. Thus, Jesus came from God for our cleansing, saying, "Unless I wash you, you have no share with me." Let us confess our sin.

Prayer of Confession

Cleanse us, Lord Jesus, as you alone are able; wash us that we may be forgiven and made whole. For we confess that, though you have commanded love and service, we are often cold and thoughtless; though you have called us to humble ministry, we have been slow to adopt the form of servants; though you have died to set us free, we have failed to show the love for one another that tells the world we belong to you and you are among us. Have mercy, O Lord, and rid us of every trace of sin. Refresh us for service and inspire us to love as you have loved us and given yourself for us. This we ask for your name's sake.

Declaration of Forgiveness
[Psalm 116:1–2, 13; 1 Corinthians 11:24–26; 1 John 1:7; 1 Peter 1:18; Hebrews 9:14]

Let us love the LORD, for he has heard our supplications. Because he has inclined his ear to us, therefore call on him your whole life long! For the cup of the new covenant is the cup of salvation, and the blood of Christ cleanses us from all sin, ransoms us from futility, purifies the conscience from dead works, and brings us near to the holy presence of God. Know that in the new covenant with Christ you are forgiven and be at peace.

Presentation of Tithes and Offerings [Psalm 116:12, 16]

The Lord has blessed us bounteously, who calls us to service, yet loosens our bonds, that the work and service we offer might be light and joyful and free. Let us show our loyalty and love for God and for one another by offering our gifts in Jesus' name.

Prayer of Dedication

Gracious God, when your Son Jesus issued the new commandment to love and gave us his humble example to follow, he said, "If you know these things, you are blessed if you do them." In that spirit, O God, and in Jesus' name, we offer these gifts, that you might sanctify them for your service. Increase in us, each day, the desire to love and serve as you command. Bless these gifts and bless us, O Lord, that they and we might be a blessing to all whom we meet, especially those to whom you would have us extend the love of Christ.

The Blessing

Show and tell the world the gospel of salvation,
and wherever you go, call on the name of the Lord!
For you are precious in God's sight,
and the Lord's eye is ever on you,
for you belong to Christ in the new covenant of the kingdom,
and you are his agents of love!

Good Friday (ABC)

Isaiah 52:12—53:12

Psalm 22

Hebrews 10:16-25 OR Hebrews 4:14-16; 5:7-9

John 18:1—19:42

IN PREPARATION FOR WORSHIP [see Psalm 22:19, 24]

O LORD, do not be far away!
Come quickly and deliver us.
For you do not despise or abhor our afflictions,
and you will not hide your face;
but surely you hear when we cry to you,
as you heard Jesus Christ from the cross,
our high priest and intercessor,
our high king and savior,
in whose name we pray.

CALL TO WORSHIP [Psalm 22:23-28]

You who fear the LORD, praise him!
All you offspring of Jacob, glorify him.
Stand in awe of him, all you offspring of Israel!
>   **All the ends of the earth shall remember and turn to the LORD.**
>   **All the families of the nations shall worship before him.**
For dominion belongs to the LORD.
God rules over the nations.
May your hearts live forever!
>   From you, O God, comes the praise of the great congregation.
>   The poor shall eat and be satisfied.
>   Those who seek him shall praise the LORD.

OPENING PRAYER [see Hebrews 4:14–16; 5:7–9]

Lord Jesus, Son of God, you are our great high priest, and, with the heavenly Father and the Holy Spirit, you are sovereign over all! Moreover, we trust in you, for you have been tested as we are tested in this world, yet you remain free from sin. In your compassion and sympathy for sinners, you cried out in prayer and supplication, and you have become the source of eternal salvation for those who love and follow you. Therefore, we approach you, our gracious Savior, with humble confidence and thankful courage, that we may receive mercy and grace to help us for our present needs and to lead us along our earthly way. May your love and truth, your suffering and death, impress us and fill us anew with passion for your mission, compassion for others, obedience to your will, and reverence for your holy name!

CALL TO CONFESSION [see Isaiah 53:8]

By a perversion of justice, the suffering servant of God was taken away. No one could have imagined his future. For he was cut off from the land of the living, stricken for our transgression. If we are to hope for justice in human affairs, then surely justice begins by addressing the highest injustice, by confessing the injustice done to God's Son, Jesus Christ. In short, justice begins with the worship of God in Jesus' name, apart from which there is no true justice. Let us therefore confess our sin, the sin that brought about the death of Christ and from which his death has set us free; by our confession we testify that the righteousness of Christ is vindicated and altogether worthy of our praise, thanksgiving, and adoration.

PRAYER OF CONFESSION [see Isaiah 52:13—53:12]

O LORD our God, we confess our sins not only for ourselves, but also for all your covenant people, past and present, and for the whole world. All we like sheep have gone astray; we have all turned to our own way, yet you laid on your Son—a man of suffering and acquainted with infirmity—the iniquity of us all. Despised and rejected, oppressed and afflicted, he did not open his mouth; like a lamb that is led to the slaughter, and like a sheep that is silent before its shearers, so he did not open his mouth. We held him of no account, but surely he has borne our infirmities and carried our diseases; he was wounded for our transgressions and crushed for our iniquities; he bore the punishment that made us whole, and by his bruises we are healed. O Lord our God, let the nations be startled and contemplate; may kings shut their mouths and consider; may all people everywhere repent and turn to you in faith, because of your servant Jesus Christ—once marred beyond human semblance, now highly exalted; Jesus Christ—once rejected, now Lord and Sovereign of all.

Declaration of Forgiveness
[see Isaiah 53:10–12; Psalm 22:29; Hebrews 5:7]

In bearing our iniquities, the righteous one Jesus Christ has made many righteous. When you consider his life an offering for sin, you are revealed as his children in the light of God and through him the will of the Lord shall prosper. Therefore, because Christ poured out himself to death and bore the sins of many, making intercession for our transgressions, to him, indeed, shall all who sleep in the earth bow down; before him shall bow all who go down to the dust, and we shall live for him. Glorify the Lord and give thanks, for by the reverent submission of Christ we have been reconciled to God.

Presentation of Tithes and Offerings [see Hebrews 10:23–25]

With faith, hope, and a pure conscience, let us urge one another to works of love in the approaching light of the eternal Day. Let us contribute our gifts in the name of Jesus for the mission of Christ and his church in the world.

Prayer of Dedication [Hebrews 10:16–25]

Holy God, by the blood of Jesus, our great high priest, you have opened a new and living way for us to approach you with confidence and assurance. For in your new covenant with Christ, you have promised not to remember our sins, and we praise you for your faithful promise that gives us hope unwavering, hearts that thirst for truth, and a deep desire henceforth to live and give faithfully according to your Word and Spirit. Receive, therefore, these expressions of our love and gratitude, that they may be used in the service of your redeeming grace and your good will, in Jesus' name.

THE BLESSING

They found no case against him, and no deceit was in his mouth.
But he came to testify to the truth,
and everyone who belongs to the truth listens to his voice.
Go, therefore, guided by the Word of truth,
empowered by the Spirit and the life-giving gospel of Jesus Christ;
tell every generation about the Lord, proclaiming his deliverance to all,
saying: the Lord has done it!

Easter (*The Resurrection of the Lord*)

Acts 10:34–43 or Isaiah 65:17–25
Psalm 118:1–2, 14–24
1 Corinthians 15:19–26 or Acts 10:34–43
John 20:1–18 or Luke 24:1–12

In Preparation for Worship

O Lord, you know our needs before we ask,
our petitions before our thoughts are fully formed:
"Before they call I will answer,
while they are yet speaking I will hear."
With such gracious provision,
your Son has faced death itself for us.
So we come to remember anew
and to give thanks for his mighty victory,
to praise you for his resurrection
and for your eternal kingdom of peace and light
that is founded upon it.
Alleluia! Praise be to God!

Call to Worship

O give thanks to the Lord, for he is good;
his steadfast love endures forever!
> The Lord is my strength and my might;
> he has become my salvation.
There are glad songs of victory in the tents of the righteous:
> the right hand of the Lord does valiantly;
> the right hand of the Lord is exalted!

I shall not die, but I shall live,
and recount the deeds of the Lord.
> The Lord has punished me severely,
> but he did not give me over to death.

This is the day that the Lord has made!
> Let us rejoice and be glad in it!

Opening Prayer

Our Lord Jesus Christ, the firstborn from the dead, you are risen from the tomb and victorious over death! You are vindicated for your sinless life, and you graciously impart to your followers the benefits of your glorious victory, by which the weeping of your people and every cry of distress shall come to an end. For you have known our greatest need and you have given your life to meet it; therefore, as your disciples fell at your feet to worship you when they first encountered you, risen from the dead, we too bow before you, and proclaim you Lord of all; to the glory of our heavenly Father, who reigns with you and the Holy Spirit, one God, now and forevermore. Amen.

Call to Confession

In the beginning, death came into the world through human sin, and in Adam all die, for it is appointed to every human being to die once. But the resurrection of the dead has also come through a human being; so all who are in Christ shall be made alive again. Let us, therefore, confess our sins that cost the Son of God his life on earth, and let us profess our hope in this same Jesus Christ, the resurrection and the life, by whom alone we are set free from our former sinful nature and from the power of death.

Prayer of Confession

Redeeming God, we confess that sin takes a great toll on our lives; it has damaged your glorious creation, compromised our health, hurt our neighbors, undermined our relationships, and separated us from full communion with you. We have often found ourselves under the power of sin, overwhelmed by its manifestations, given in to despair. Forgive us, Lord. For you are not overcome by the world, but in Christ Jesus you have overcome the world! You make all things new: new heavens, a new earth, and each forgiven sinner a new creation in Christ! Grant us

such an outpouring of your grace as to cleanse us thoroughly from our sin, and raise us with Christ into new life, that we may henceforth live in the light of the good news of the resurrection, unafraid of death, and boldly going forth to proclaim your righteousness, your goodness, and your truth.

Declaration of Forgiveness

Hear the good news! Jesus Christ has been raised from the dead, the first fruits of those who have died. All the prophets testify about him that everyone who believes in him receives forgiveness of sins through his name. He shall reign until he has put all his enemies under his feet, and the last enemy to be destroyed is death. Then, the former things shall not be remembered or come to mind. But be glad and rejoice forever in what the Lord is creating; for you, the people of God, shall be a joy and a delight, prosperous and at peace. Know that in Christ you are not only forgiven, but you are an entirely new creation. Alleluia! Thanks be God!

Presentation of Tithes and Offerings

Friends, since God raised Jesus on the third day and allowed him to appear, not to all the people, but to those who were chosen to serve as witnesses, so we too have the responsibility to convey the gospel to this generation. Surely we have no greater gift than to share the message of the gospel: the forgiveness of sins and the resurrection to eternal life that we have in Jesus Christ. Let us offer our gifts in the service of this good news.

Prayer of Dedication

We thank you, O Lord,
for the marvelous things you have done in Jesus Christ,
who, though once rejected, is now risen from the dead.
Jesus has become our salvation, and he is Lord of all.
Accept, we pray, these gifts of gratitude, offered in joy,
that their use may indeed, by the power of the Holy Spirit,
serve the proclamation of your glorious gospel of peace
and eternal life in Christ.

The Charge and Blessing

Look not for the living among the dead,
but serve Christ until the end,
when, having overcome every ruler, power, and authority,
he shall hand over the kingdom to God the Father.
Seek the kingdom of your resurrected Lord,
knowing that the sound of weeping shall be heard in it no more,
neither shall the cry of distress.
For like the days of a tree shall the days of God's people be,
and the chosen shall long enjoy the work of their hands.
You shall not labor in vain, or bear children for calamity;
but in Christ you are all offspring blessed by the Lord.

Easter Evening (ABC)

Isaiah 25:6–9

Psalm 114

1 Corinthians 5:6b–8

Luke 24:13–49

IN PREPARATION FOR WORSHIP

For generations your people have remembered
the release from captivity, the liberation from slavery,
the exodus from Egypt.
Then, again in a time of oppression, the resurrection!
Jesus Christ, slain as a lamb at the Passover,
arose from the dead and departed the tomb.
The greatest enemy, the most oppressive power—
death—is thus defeated.
O meet with us once again, Lord Jesus.
Restore what is lacking in our faith
and speak that we may burn ever brighter with hope.

CALL TO WORSHIP [1 Corinthians 5:7b–8; Luke 24:30–34]

Christ our paschal lamb has been sacrificed.
> **Let us therefore keep the feast**
> **with the unleavened bread of sincerity and truth.**

Christ the bread of life has risen from the dead!
> **Let us celebrate the festival**
> **in the presence of our risen Lord.**

Christ the Lord has risen indeed!
> **Let us attend anew to the living Word.**
> **Let us open the Scriptures and listen to the LORD.**

Opening Prayer

Eternal God, how wondrous it is that our Lord Jesus, having suffered for our sins, has risen from the grave and entered into his glory! Surely the whole creation will never be the same, for you, the Lord of life, have overthrown the finality of death! Come, O Lord, and bless us as we search the Scriptures, remember your mighty deeds, bask in your presence, partake of your provision, and discern your will, that we may offer you the adoration of our hearts and the witness of our lives.

Call to Confession [see 1 Corinthians 5:6b–8]

As those who prepared to leave behind the slavery of Egypt rid themselves of yeast, let us likewise make ready for pure and faithful discipleship; let us clean out the old leaven of sin and evil, doubt and rebellion, bitterness and ill will, by confessing our sin to the One who alone can make us entirely new.

Prayer of Confession [Luke 24:25–27, 32, 45]

Holy God, you are the giver and the restorer of life! From the beginning you have revealed the redeeming mission of your Messiah to your prophets and your people of faith; yet apart from faith, it has remained concealed. Where sin and doubt have taken hold, our hearts and minds have been blinded and our spirits have grown slothful and dull. Forgive us, O Lord, for our foolish and unfaithful ways. Restore us in heart, mind, and spirit, that we may be receptive to your presence, your gospel, and your purpose for us, and that we may be trustworthy bearers of your glad and joyful news to those who remain in the grip of doubt, despair, and darkness.

Declaration of Forgiveness [see Psalm 114:8; Isaiah 25:7–9b]

The Lord—who turns rock and flint into pools and streams of water—the Lord has spoken. God has promised to swallow up death forever, to wipe away the tears from all faces, and to take the disgrace from his people, indeed, from all the earth. This is the Lord for whom we have waited; let us be glad and rejoice in his salvation; for in the risen Lord Jesus Christ, we are forgiven.

Easter Evening (ABC)

Presentation of Tithes and Offerings [see Isaiah 25:6–9]

God has promised that with the death of death itself, with the destruction of the shroud that is cast over the nations, he shall in its place provide a feast of rich food and clear, well-aged wines. In anticipation of that future day, let us share our gifts and provisions, that a foretaste, however simple and humble, of that coming feast may be seen in our midst and that the invitation to others might go forth from this place in Jesus' name.

Prayer of Dedication

Almighty God, the whole creation rejoices at the victory of Jesus Christ over death! The mountains and hills, the seas and the rivers delight at your sovereign power and your holy presence! Moreover, your Spirit has called us to be your witnesses to these things, to proclaim in your name that the Messiah is risen and that repentance and the forgiveness of sins are decreed for all nations. To that end, we present these gifts for the sake of your commission, for the work of your church, and for the glory of your risen Son, in whose name we pray.

The Blessing

Bear the good news into the world, the invitation to the feast of Christ!
Tell the nations that death is defeated and the promise of God for life is sure.
For Christ is risen! Forgiveness is given! The Lord of life awaits our return.
May your hearts burn with the assurance of his presence
and may the Spirit empower you with truth and love.

Second Sunday of Easter

Acts 5:27–32

Psalm 118:14–29 OR Psalm 150

Revelation 1:4–8

John 20:19–31

IN PREPARATION FOR WORSHIP

God of the Resurrection,
give us minds to believe what cannot be seen
and hearts to trust what cannot be held;
refresh us now with the great gifts
of repentance, and faith, and your Holy Spirit,
that our lives may be conformed to your holy will.

CALL TO WORSHIP

Praise the LORD!
Praise God in his sanctuary;
praise him in his mighty firmament!
> **Praise him for his mighty deeds;**
> **praise him according to his surpassing greatness!**

Praise him with trumpet sound;
praise him with lute and harp!
> **Praise him with tambourine and dance;**
> **praise him with strings and pipe!**

Praise him with clanging cymbals;
praise him with loud clashing cymbals!
> **Let everything that breathes praise the LORD!**
> **Praise the LORD!**

Opening Prayer

O Lord,
this is the day that you have made, the day of resurrection;
you are our strength and our might;
and your Son Jesus Christ has become our salvation.
Open the gates of righteousness
that your people may enter through them,
with joy and gladness,
to give you thanks and praise.
Hear our glad songs of victory within your tabernacle,
for your right hand has done valiantly
in raising our Lord Jesus Christ from the dead.
Hallelujah! Thanks be to God!

Call to Confession

"Look! Christ is coming with the clouds! Every eye will see him, even those who pierced him, and on his account all the tribes of the earth will wail!" Through Jesus, the way has been opened for us to repent—for repentance is a gift!—and to receive the forgiveness of sins, and by the power of the Holy Spirit we have been given authority to forgive! Let us confess our sins to God and receive cleansing by the blood of Christ, that we might also become agents of reconciliation in Jesus' name.

Prayer of Confession

O God of our ancestors, we confess that we have often sequestered ourselves in fear, harbored foolish doubts, paid greater deference to human authority than to your own, and forgotten your mighty deeds done in past generations. Forgive us, O God, and make us ever mindful of your purpose in sending Jesus Christ to suffer and die for us; may all the signs that you have performed foster ever greater faith in our hearts, throughout your church, and in those who have not yet come to believe, that all who come to faith in Jesus as Messiah may have life in his name.

Declaration of Forgiveness

Do not doubt, but believe! For by believing that Jesus is the Christ, you have life in his name! Be assured that the faithful witness Jesus Christ loves us and has freed us from our sins by means of his blood. The One who is firstborn from the dead and ruler of all the kings of the earth has made us a kingdom of priests to serve his God and Father forever! Glory be to God, the Alpha and the Omega, who is and who was and who is to come!

Presentation of Tithes and Offerings

The Lord is God, and he has given us light.
For such is the marvelous revelation of God:
that Christ Jesus, though rejected by human authorities,
has become the chief cornerstone of saving faith.
Blessed is the one who comes in the name of the Lord!
Let us offer thanksgiving to the Lord,
whose steadfast love endures forever.

Prayer of Dedication

O Lord our God, you are exceedingly good;
we give you thanks and extol you,
for you answer the prayers of your people with salvation and blessing.
Grant us success, O Lord, we beseech you,
that in giving, we may imitate and exalt Jesus Christ,
and in living, we may recount and witness to
the mighty deeds of your Holy Spirit.

The Charge and Blessing

Peace be with you, in the name of Jesus Christ!
As God the Father has sent Jesus Christ,
so the Father and the Son send the Holy Spirit upon the church.
Receive, therefore, the Holy Spirit,
that you may exercise discernment, proclaim forgiveness,
and witness to the resurrection of Jesus.
Blessed are you who have not yet seen the risen Lord,
but have come to believe in him;
and blessed shall they be who come to believe
through your witness, and the testimony of the whole church.

Third Sunday of Easter

Acts 9:1–6 (7–20)

Psalm 30

Revelation 5:11–14

John 21:1–19

In Preparation for Worship

God of Glory,
restore my sight that I may see you,
revive my heart that I may hear you,
and rekindle my faith that I may love you fully,
that you might do something extraordinary,
even with this humble servant.

Call to Worship

I looked and heard the voice of many angels
surrounding the throne and the hosts of heaven singing,
> **"Worthy is the Lamb who was slain**
> **to receive power and wealth and wisdom and might**
> **and honor and glory and blessing!"**

Then I heard every creature in heaven, and on the earth,
and under the earth, and in the seas, singing,
> **"To the One seated on the throne and to the Lamb**
> **be blessing and honor and glory and might**
> **forever and ever!"**

And the four living creatures said,
> **"Amen!"**

And the elders fell down and worshiped.
> **Let us worship God.**

Opening Prayer

Holy God,
you have called your church
to tell of the resurrection of Jesus Christ,
and to declare your name before the nations and their leaders.
Nurture us, we pray, by your sustaining word,
that we may regain our strength for service.
Grant us endurance, that we may persevere in faith,
for the sake of your name,
proclaiming Jesus to this generation,
for truly, "He is the Son of God!"

Call to Confession

Repentance can take many forms, from the decisive and dramatic to the subtle and gradual, but all must appear before the Lord Jesus Christ. Therefore, let us be washed, clothed, and converted; let us express our repentance in a moment of confession, confident that Christ himself repeatedly renews his disciples, granting new strength and new vision to those who approach him in humility.

Prayer of Confession

By your favor, O Lord, you established your church in the strength of your Spirit; yet we confess that in times of prosperity, we grow complacent, and in times of trouble, when you hide your face, we soon despair. To you, O Lord, we make our supplication: hear us, O Lord, and be gracious. O Lord, be our helper and forgive our sins. For you have called us to praise you and to tell of your faithfulness. Surely there is no praise or profit for you in the dust of the Pit. Therefore, we will extol you, O Lord, for, in Christ and with Christ, you have drawn us up. Do not let our foes rejoice over us. To you we have cried, and you have healed us. You have raised us from the depths of Sheol, and restored us to life.

Declaration of Forgiveness

Friends in Christ, may the gracious hand of God rest upon you,
and the risen Lord speak peace to your troubled hearts, saying,
"Open your eyes, regain your sight, and be filled with the Holy Spirit."

Be restored in your faith, renewed in your calling,
and reestablished in the baptimal covenant,
for, in Jesus Christ, we are forgiven.

OR

Sing praises to the LORD, O you his faithful ones,
and give thanks to his holy name.
For his anger is but for a moment;
his favor is for a lifetime.
Weeping may linger for the night,
but joy comes with the morning.
May the LORD turn your mourning into dancing,
taking off your sackcloth and clothing you with joy,
so that you may praise the LORD and not be silent.
O LORD our God, we will give thanks to you forever!

Presentation of Tithes and Offerings

We, like Jesus' first disciples, are commissioned to fish for people. Yet we, like the first disciples, can catch nothing apart from the presence and the direction of our risen Lord, Christ. With Christ, however, we have every reason to hope for profitable labor and full nets. Having been fed by the Word and renewed in the Spirit, let us offer to the Lord what provisions we have, that in his wisdom, he might bless them and guide us in their use to an abundant harvest.

Prayer of Dedication

O Lord our God, receive this portion of our provisions, offered in Jesus' name; bless and increase them, and direct their use and distribution, according to your gracious will and for your glory.

The Charge and Blessing

Go in the love of Christ,
to feed his lambs,
to tend his flock,
to nurture his sheep,
for the time is hastening on.

Therefore, serve the Lord Jesus with gladness,
in every moment of every day,
who calls you, even now, saying,
"Follow me."

Fourth Sunday of Easter

Acts 9:36–43
Psalm 23
Revelation 7:9–17
John 10:22–30

In Preparation for Worship

Good Shepherd,
attune my ears to hear your voice;
call me that I may follow;
grant me eternal fellowship with you,
that we may ever be one.

Call to Worship

After this I looked and saw a great multitude that no one could count,
from every nation and people and language and culture,
standing before the throne and before the Lamb, robed in white,
and crying in a loud voice, saying,
> "Salvation belongs to our God
> who is seated on the throne, and to the Lamb!"

These are those who have come out of the great tribulation;
they have washed their robes and made them white in the blood of the Lamb.
> **They worship the Lord day and night,**
> **and the One who sits on the throne shelters them.**

They will hunger and thirst no more. Neither will the sun strike them.
For the Lamb is the Lord and the Lord is their Shepherd!
> **The Lord will guide us to springs of living water.**
> **God will wipe away every tear from our eyes.**

Opening Prayer

Shepherd Lord,
lead us in your righteous paths for your name's sake;
restore our weary souls; anoint us with your Spirit;
fill us to overflowing with your water of life;
and surround us with goodness and mercy,
that we may dwell in your house forever.

Call to Confession

Do your words and your works, your thoughts and your actions, speak to the world of your faith in God? Or does your need to control override your obedience? Do you trust that the Lord has your salvation well in hand, or do you suspect God of being just another god? Come, let us unburden ourselves in confession.

Prayer of Confession

**God of the Resurrection,
we cannot save ourselves by our good works, initiative, or cleverness.
You alone have power to conquer sin and raise the dead.
We confess we have doubted your willingness to heal us,
forgotten how faithfully you have cleansed us in the past,
and failed to develop the mighty gifts you have given us
and charged us to use on behalf of others.
Forgive us, O God, and renew our lives
that we might stir others to seek new life in you.**

Declaration of Forgiveness

Hear the words of our Lord Jesus Christ:
"My sheep hear my voice. I know them, and they follow me.
I give them eternal life, and they will never perish.
No one will ever snatch them out of my hand."
As the Lord is your Shepherd, so you belong to Christ:
you are forgiven, and your salvation is secure in the hands of God.

Presentation of Tithes and Offerings

With the Lord as our shepherd we shall not want for anything. The eternal God promises us eternal life, on top of ample provisions for this life. How then shall we respond to God's goodness and mercy, if not with humble thanks and acts of charity, generosity, and love?

Prayer of Dedication

Salvation is yours, O God, and we too are yours.
Without your creating us for your glory, we would not exist.
Without your reconciling us to yourself, we would be cut off.
Without the gift of your Spirit, we would wither and die.
Therefore, we offer you our all:
body, mind, and spirit; thought, speech, and action;
hearts raised in devotion, souls praising your worth,
and arms uplifting these blessings that we return to you.

The Charge and Blessing

Let the Good Shepherd guide you out of your life's ruts and routines
and into God's paths of righteousness.
Attend to and follow the familiar voice of the Shepherd.
Drink deeply and be filled with the Holy Spirit,
that you may be a channel for God's blessings,
overflowing with the water of life.

Fifth Sunday of Easter

Acts 11:1–18

Psalm 148

Revelation 21:1–6

John 13:31–35

In Preparation for Worship

Loving God,
you haved commanded us to love,
so that the world will know by our love
that we belong to you.
Fill us with love,
for such love as you command
may be found nowhere else than with you;
indeed, you are love.

Call to Worship

Praise the Lord from the heavens!
Praise God in the heights above!
> **Praise the Lord, all you angels!**
> **Praise God all you heavenly hosts!**

Praise the Lord, sun and moon!
Praise God, all you shining stars!
> **Praise the Lord, you mountains and hills, you beasts and cattle!**
> **Praise God, you creatures of the deep, you flying birds!**

Praise the Lord, O kings of the earth!
Praise God, young and old, every man and every woman!

Let everyone praise the LORD, for God's name alone is holy!
The glory of the LORD is above all the earth!
Let all the faithful praise the LORD!

Opening Prayer

Spirit of God, we praise you that you are not bound by our shortsighted understanding of categories that you alone define. We thank you that your baptism not only cleanses us with water but also fills us with joy, endows us with gifts, and empowers us with the talents that are all part of our new life in Christ. May this new life fill our hearts, flow through our lives, nurture our families, our community, your church, and your world, all in the Spirit of your Love.

Call to Confession

God is preparing for us a new heaven and a new earth, with the holy city, Jerusalem, for its capital. But to live there entails preparation. Do we not prepare ourselves for even the shortest errand or outing? Surely, then, the ultimate journey to God's heavenly kingdom warrants a lifetime of preparation, for it is a journey that begins with baptism and continues into the eternal life beyond this life. How do we prepare ourselves for this great journey? We alone cannot. Our part is to honestly admit we are sinners and to continually turn from sin. Let us ask God's forgiveness for past sins and for divine help in preparing us for life in the present and coming kingdom.

Prayer of Confession

Eternal God,
we confess that we have failed to love as you have loved us,
and we are worthy of punishment for our many sins.
We thirst for the water of life,
for your righteous Spirit imparted to us.
Without you, O God, we would die.
Make your home among us now,
and fashion us into your forgiven people,
that the world might look to us
and see your family sharing in the abundance
of your infinite mercy and your steadfast love.

Declaration of Forgiveness

The One who is seated on the throne of heaven says, "See, I am making all things new." What God has made clean, others must not call profane. This does not mean such categories no longer exist, but simply that God, who baptizes with the Holy Spirit, gives the repentance that leads to life and the gift of faith in Jesus Christ to whom he will; thus we shall not hinder God's grace or make distinctions where God does not. Give praise to God, whose home is among mortals, who will wipe every tear from our eyes. "Death will be no more; mourning and crying and pain will be no more, for the first things have passed away." Know that you are forgiven and be at peace.

Presentation of Tithes and Offerings

Jesus has given us a new commandment, that we should love one another. For he has said, "Just as I have loved you, you also should love one another. By this everyone will know that you are my disciples, if you have love for one another." Let us, therefore, offer gifts to God in the spirit of love, that they may be used in love for the care of Christ's church, and to demonstrate to the world the glorious presence of Christ in the midst of his people. Let us offer our gifts to the glory of God.

Prayer of Dedication

Lord Jesus Christ,
you are the Alpha and the Omega,
the beginning and the end,
and your words are trustworthy and true.
You graciously grant the water of life as a gift to all those who thirst.
Use these gifts, we pray, that they may bring relief in your name
to those in need of your living word and your life-giving truth;
we offer them for the sake of your sovereign will.

The Charge and Blessing

May the Holy Spirit rest upon and direct you,
ever bringing to mind the word of the Lord,
the gospel by which those who have not yet heard will be saved.
Go forth in love, fulfilling Christ's command,
proclaiming the good news for the praise of God's glory!

Sixth Sunday of Easter

Acts 16:9–15

Psalm 67

Revelation 21:10; 21:22—22:5

John 14:23–29 OR John 5:1–9

IN PREPARATION FOR WORSHIP

Lord Jesus, your word from the Father
is the promise of love and abiding fellowship with you.
Mindful of your love, we in turn offer you our love,
for we believe and would hold fast to your word.
Therefore, meet us in worship, we pray;
secure love everlastingly in our hearts
and establish our understanding of your word,
that we may recall it faithfully by the grace of your Spirit,
never fearing disappointment or surrendering to despair.

CALL TO WORSHIP

May your way may be known upon earth, O God,
your saving power among all nations.
> **Let the peoples praise you, O God;**
> **let all the peoples praise you.**

Let the nations be glad and sing for joy,
for you judge the peoples with equity
and guide the nations upon earth.
> **Let the peoples praise you, O God;**
> **let all the peoples praise you.**

Opening Prayer

O God our Heavenly Father,
we rejoice that our Savior, the risen Lord Jesus,
is now with you on high, just as he foretold.
As we await his final return, send your Holy Spirit upon your church,
that our Advocate might teach us everything that you, O God,
Father, Son, and Holy Spirit, desire us to know,
and remind us of all that your living Word has said to us.

Call to Confession

Jesus said, "Whoever does not love me does not keep my words." Sin, then, is not merely a failure of memory or of obedience, but it is ultimately a deficiency in our love for Christ. When presented with an opportunity for healing, therefore, let us not seek in our ailments an excuse for remaining as we are, but let us trust and obey the one who asks us in love, "Do you want to be healed?" and who commands us to arise and walk in the newness of life. Let us confess our sin, trusting that the Christ who promises us new life offers to renew our love as well.

Prayer of Confession

Lord God Almighty, you have revealed that the gates of your holy city will ever be open, for they will never be shut by day—and there will be no night there. Yet, the new Jerusalem will admit nothing accursed or unclean and no one who practices abomination or falsehood. We confess we long for such a place, for we are weary of worldliness, of subtle deceptions, of outright lies, of sins we see committed around us and those we see in ourselves. Forgive us, we pray, for all our iniquities, and release us especially from those sins that have a greater grip on us than we have mastery over them. Prepare our hearts, minds, souls, and bodies to worship you aright, to offer you our gifts, to bring you honor, and to dwell in your glorious light; may we each be written, by the light of his lamp, into the Lamb's book of Life; for it is in Jesus' name that we pray.

Declaration of Forgiveness

Jesus said, "Peace I leave with you; my peace I give to you.
I do not give to you as the world gives.
Do not let your hearts be troubled, and do not let them be afraid."

For this same Jesus, the Lamb of God,
who promises the Holy Spirit, gives the Spirit,
like a river flowing with the water of life, crystal clear,
from the throne of God.
This river waters the tree of life, to which in Christ we have access,
the tree whose leaves are for the healing of the nations.
Friends, remember that you are baptized:
you bear the name of Christ and the redeeming mark of the Holy Spirit;
the Lord God is your light and you are God's forgiven people,
who shall reign with God forever and ever.

Presentation of Tithes and Offerings

How shall we act in keeping with the prayers we have spoken, with the Word we have heard, and with the Lord who has opened our hearts? How shall we respond in accordance with our baptism? Let us offer the Lord our gifts, showing our desire to be hospitable to Christ, open to the movement of the Spirit and supporting the church's mission.

Prayer of Dedication

You, O God, are a God on a mission,
calling your servants and inspiring us with visions of
how you would have us pray,
what you would have us do,
where you would have us labor,
and to whom you would have us proclaim the good news.
Bless and apply these gifts, we pray, in keeping with your purpose,
that they may be used and bear fruit accordingly,
giving glory to the name of Jesus Christ
wherever you would open human hearts to your Word.

The Charge and Blessing

May God be gracious to us and bless us
and make his face to shine upon us.
The earth has yielded its increase;
God, our God, has blessed us.
May God continue to bless us;
let all the ends of the earth revere him.

Ascension of the Lord (ABC)

Acts 1:1–11
Psalm 47 OR Psalm 93
Ephesians 1:15–23
Luke 24:44–53

IN PREPARATION FOR WORSHIP

Heavenly Father,
there is much we do not know
regarding all that you do in your sovereign power.
But we know you are gracious and swift to send your Spirit
to those who wait for you with joy and eager expectation.
Thus, we gather; in joy, we wait.
May our worship exalt your ascended Son,
and brim with your Holy Spirit.

CALL TO WORSHIP [Psalms 47:1–2, 6–7; 93:3–4]

Clap your hands, all you peoples.
Shout to God with loud songs of joy.
> For the LORD, the Most High, is awesome,
> a great king over all the earth.
Sing praises to God, sing praises.
Sing praises to our King, sing praises.
> For God is the king of all the earth.
> Sing praises with a psalm.
The floods have lifted up, O LORD,
the floods have lifted up their voice.
> More majestic than the waves of the sea,
> majestic on high is the LORD!

Opening Prayer [see Ephesians 1:15–23]

Eternal God, your power is immeasurable and your heritage rich and glorious! What is more, you have given your people the gift of faith in Christ Jesus through whom you put your power to work, reveal your wisdom, and illumine our hearts. We thank you that we have such a gracious redeemer, who is now seated at your right hand and reigns with you and the Holy Spirit as one God, far above all rule and authority and power and dominion, and above every name, not only in this age but also in the age to come. All praise to you, our triune God!

Call to Confession [Psalms 47:8; 93:1–2, 5]

God sits on his holy throne and rules over the nations. The LORD has established the world, that it should never be moved. Indeed, the LORD is the everlasting God and his decrees are very sure. Yet who among us can claim to have lived, without fail, according to the LORD's commands? Surely it was for fallen humanity that the Messiah died and rose again and ascended into his glory. Let us confess our sin.

Prayer of Confession

God of glory, we confess that, although you call your people to holy living, we have failed to keep our hearts and minds free of the profane things of this world; we presume to know more than we do, we speak rashly, and, forgetful that Jesus Christ alone is head of the church, we judge others harshly, thereby risking our own condemnation. Forgive us, O Lord, and give us a spirit of wisdom and revelation as we come to know you, that the eyes of our hearts might be enlightened with your gracious presence and with the hope to which you have called us in Christ Jesus our Lord.

Declaration of Forgiveness

On the day Jesus was taken up, he charged his followers with proclaiming repentance and the forgiveness of sins to all nations. Today, that message remains unaltered. It is the word we are to both hear and tell abroad. In Jesus Christ, we are forgiven! Therefore, let us turn to him, exalt and expect him, and bless his name in every circumstance, wherever his Spirit leads us.

Presentation of Tithes and Offerings

Mindful of the mission of God and the needs of the saints, thankful for all the riches of God's glorious inheritance in Christ, let us offer tithes and offerings and alms, that they too might be lifted up for the glory of God and sent forth for the service of our sovereign Lord.

Prayer of Dedication

O God, you are highly exalted, and we rejoice that you have made your risen Son the head over all things for the church. Truly, you have placed all things under his feet, for he has ascended to the right hand of power and he alone is worthy to reign with you. Bless the saints, we pray, and bless these offerings; bless us all with the fullness of Christ, that the church, as his body, might fill the whole creation, and that your faithful, penitent, hopeful, and loving people might cause the whole earth to resound with the praise of your name.

The Blessing

You are witnesses of Christ,
of all that he is and of all that he does,
of all that he has done and all that he has promised to do
for the restoration of all things.
One day he shall return, just as he left,
but for now you are witnesses,
empowered by the Spirit, equipped for every good work,
and sent forth with blessing, a blessing undiminished by his ascension,
but increased as it comes from on high.
Go in the power of his blessing,
and bear witness to Christ's gracious death,
his resurrection, and his glorious ascension
until he comes again.

Seventh Sunday of Easter

Acts 16:16–34

Psalm 97

Revelation 22:12–14, 16–17, 20–21

John 17:20–26

IN PREPARATION FOR WORSHIP

The Spirit and the bride say, "Come."
And let everyone who hears say, "Come."
And let everyone who is thirsty come.
Let anyone who wishes take the water of life as a gift.
As the Lord Jesus has promised, "Surely I am coming soon,"
so we say, "Amen. Come, Lord Jesus!"

CALL TO WORSHIP

The Lord is king! Let the earth rejoice;
let the many coastlands be glad!
> Clouds and thick darkness are all around him;
> righteousness and justice are the foundation of his throne.
Fire goes before him,
and consumes his adversaries on every side.
> His lightnings light up the world;
> the earth sees and trembles.
The mountains melt like wax before the Lord,
before the Lord of all the earth.
> The heavens proclaim his righteousness;
> and all the peoples behold his glory.

Opening Prayer

Almighty God, who breaks the chains of prisoners and shatters the bars of confinement when your servants but turn to you in worship and exalt your name in song: draw us and those who do not yet know you into this circle of worship and fellowship, that your Spirit of baptism might bring new life and that whole households might be saved, confessing the name of the Lord Jesus Christ, who is the first and the last, the beginning and the end, the root, the Son of David, and the bright morning star.

Call to Confession

The psalmist declares,
"All worshipers of images are put to shame,
those who make their boast in worthless idols;
but all gods bow down before the Lord."
Friends, let us believe on the Lord Jesus,
with the full assurance that those who do so will be saved.
For blessed are those who wash their robes,
so that they will have the right to the tree of life
and may enter the city of God by its gates.
Let us confess our sins to God.

Prayer of Confession

God of peace, we confess that we have made war, created strife, and stirred conflict in the world and in our hearts. Have mercy. Spirit of unity, we confess that we have divided your church, perpetuated schisms, and broken your heart. Have mercy. O Truth that gives freedom, we confess that we speak highly of freedom, but shackle ourselves to material goods, selfish aims, and private ambitions. Have mercy. Forgive us for our sins, and reveal your kingdom anew among us, free of fighting, free of schism, free of enslavement to sin. We ask this in the name of our Lord Jesus Christ, our Prince of Peace.

Declaration of Forgiveness

Hear and be glad, O people.
Rejoice at the gracious judgments of God.
For the Lord is most high over all the earth,
exalted far above all gods.

The LORD loves those who hate evil;
he guards the lives of his faithful;
he rescues them from the hand of the wicked.
See now how light dawns for the righteous,
and joy for the upright in heart!
For in Christ you are forgiven and made righteous,
and all the blessings of righteousness are yours.
Rejoice in the LORD, O you righteous,
and give thanks to his holy name!

Presentation of Tithes and Offerings

When Jesus prayed for his followers to be one, he also prayed for us, for those who would come to believe through the testimony of the apostles, just as we have done. Knowing that we and the whole church have no less an intercessor than the Lord Jesus, praying that the whole world might come to faith through our witness, let us offer what gifts we have set apart for this mission, that the unity of the church might be seen, and thus render glory to our triune God.

Prayer of Dedication

Righteous Father,
though the world does not know you,
we are blessed to know you through Jesus Christ,
whom you have sent.
Help us, we pray, to make your name known to the world,
and use these gifts for that very purpose,
so that the love that you and your Son have shown your church
may be revealed in the church and throughout the world.
This we ask on behalf of all who will come to believe in Jesus
through the witness of your people,
that we may all be one in Christ Jesus
by the power of the Holy Spirit.

The Charge and Blessing

Friends, it is our Lord Jesus
who has given his testimony to the church, saying,
"See, I am coming soon; my reward is with me,

to repay according to everyone's work."
Let your work, therefore, be your worship,
and your worship your work,
that in your prayers and praises
the Spirit might open doors
to the mighty works of God.
And may the grace of the Lord Jesus
be with all the saints. Amen.

Pentecost

Acts 2:1–21 OR Genesis 11:1–9
Psalm 104:24–34, 35b
Romans 8:14–17 OR Acts 2:1–21
John 14:8–17 (25–27)

In Preparation for Worship

Holy God,
we have heard your Word speak,
we have seen your Spirit work,
and we know that you abide
in the living Lord Jesus.
Bring to mind all that you have revealed;
fill our hearts with the breath of your Spirit;
enable us to know you and to witness to you
in truth and love.

Call to Worship

May the glory of the Lord endure forever;
may the Lord rejoice in his works—
>who looks on the earth and it trembles,
>who touches the mountains and they smoke.

I will sing to the Lord as long as I live;
I will sing praise to my God while I have being.
>**May my meditation be pleasing to him,**
>**for I rejoice in the Lord.**

Bless the Lord, O my soul.
>**Praise the Lord!**

Opening Prayer

Here we are, O Lord,
gathered in this place, in Jesus' name.
Come, Holy Spirit! Come down from heaven.
Fill this house of prayer and show yourself among us.
Rest upon each one, make each heart burn within,
and enable us to worship you aright.
Let no one mistake our inspiration, but let everyone know
that your Spirit is with us and among us,
empowering your church to testify in these last days,
that everyone who calls on the name of the Lord shall be saved.

Call to Confession

You did not receive a spirit of slavery to fall back into fear, but you have received a spirit of adoption from the Holy Spirit, the Advocate, who teaches and reminds you of all that Jesus Christ has said to you, and who gives repentance itself as a gift. Jesus has promised that this same Holy Spirit, apart from whom we are not even able to confess our sins, will be with us and will abide in us forever. This is the Spirit of truth, whom the world cannot receive, because it neither sees him nor knows him; but you know him. Therefore, with the Spirit's guidance and strength, let us confess our sins to God.

Prayer of Confession

Holy and eternal God, we confess that we have failed to keep your commandments; we have been quick to surrender our dreams and visions, and slow to share in the sufferings of Christ; we are too easily bound by fear and reluctant to surrender those things in our lives that block the free flow of your mighty love. Forgive us, O God, and clear a straight path from your mouth to our hearts, that our lives might overflow with the good news of your grace that we see and know in Jesus Christ.

Declaration of Forgiveness [John 14:27; 8:15–17]

Jesus said, "Peace I leave with you; my peace I give to you.
I do not give to you as the world gives.
Do not let your hearts be troubled, and do not let them be afraid."
And the Apostle Paul has assured us

that "all who are led by the Spirit of God are children of God.
When we cry, 'Abba! Father!' it is that very Spirit
bearing witness with our spirit that we are children of God,
and if children, then heirs of God and joint heirs with Christ."
Friends, know that in Christ we are forgiven,
in faith we have the gift of the Spirit,
and in the Spirit, we have the promise of new life.

Presentation of Tithes and Offerings [John 14:12–14]

Jesus promised, "Very truly, I tell you, the one who believes in me will also do the works that I do and, in fact, will do greater works than these, because I am going to the Father. I will do whatever you ask in my name, so that the Father may be glorified in the Son. If in my name you ask me for anything, I will do it." Therefore, let us place our gifts at God's disposal, that they may be used in the power of the Holy Spirit to do great things for the glory of our triune God.

Prayer of Dedication [Psalm 104:24, 27–30]

"O Lord, how manifold are your works!
In wisdom you have made them all;
the earth is full of your creatures.
These all look to you
to give them their food in due season;
when you give to them, they gather it up;
when you open your hand, they are filled with good things.
When you hide your face, they are dismayed;
when you take away their breath, they die
and return to their dust.
When you send forth your Spirit, they are created;
and you renew the face of the ground."
Send forth your Spirit upon these gifts, we pray,
that with them you might do marvelous things,
and thus manifest the glory of your creative and renewing ways
to this weary world.

The Charge and Blessing

Friends, you belong to none other than the triune God.

Therefore, let your hearts be filled with the fire of God's Spirit.
Let your hearts burn with the love of God's Truth.
Let your searching eyes seek the face of Jesus,
knowing and sharing the knowledge that
God is revealed and dwells fully in Christ,
in whom alone salvation has come.

PART III

Ordinary Time (Propers 4–29)
Trinity—All Saints'—Christ the King

Trinity Sunday

Proverbs 8:1–4, 22–31
Psalm 8
Romans 5:1–5
John 16:12–15

IN PREPARATION FOR WORSHIP

When you established the heavens, O God, Wisdom was there;
when you drew a circle on the face of the deep,
Wisdom was beside you, like a master worker,
rejoicing before you always, rejoicing in your inhabited world.
Grant us wisdom, O LORD; grant us your spirit of wisdom,
that we may worship and delight in you
and in all that you have created for your glory.

CALL TO WORSHIP

O LORD, our Sovereign,
how majestic is your name in all the earth!
You have set your glory above the heavens.
> Out of the mouths of babes and infants
> you have founded a bulwark because of your foes,
> to silence the enemy and the avenger.
When I look at your heavens, the work of your fingers,
the moon and the stars that you have established;
> what are human beings that you are mindful of them,
> mortals that you care for them?
Yet you have made them a little lower than God,
and crowned them with glory and honor.

>> You have given them dominion over the works of your hands;
>> you have put all things under their feet,
> all sheep and oxen, and also the beasts of the field,
> the birds of the air, and the fish of the sea,
> whatever passes along the paths of the seas.
>> O LORD, our Sovereign,
>> how majestic is your name in all the earth!

OPENING PRAYER

Spirit of truth, come and guide your church into all the truth; speak to us what you have heard, and declare the things that are to come. May your revelation of the Word of God, and our response in worship and works of love, give glory to the Word made flesh and to the heavenly Father, who has given all things into the hands of Jesus the Christ, the Son of God, in whose name we pray.

CALL TO CONFESSION

The voice of God's wisdom cries out to all people and to every living creature, calling at the very portals of the heart: God has crowned you with glory and honor! What are your sufferings by comparison? Should these not produce endurance, and character, and hope? Setting aside all thought of disappointment, let us confess our sins to our gracious God.

PRAYER OF CONFESSION

Sovereign LORD, what are human beings that you are mindful of us? You have given us dominion over your creation, yet we have exploited what you have entrusted to us. You have revealed to us the wisdom through which you created the world and with which you designed its very fabric, yet we have foolishly sought other explanations, causes, and powers to appear wiser and more capable than we are. Forgive us, O God, for our sins and for our foolish, self-seeking ways. Let us no longer seek a lesser glory than your own, no longer act or think or speak in such ways as diminish the majesty of your name.

Declaration of Forgiveness

Friends, since we are justified by faith—
faith enacted as repentance; faith that is the opposite of sin—
we now have peace with God through our Lord Jesus Christ,
through whom we have obtained access
to this very grace in which we now stand.
Believers in Christ,
know that you are forgiven, and be at peace.

Presentation of Tithes and Offerings

Surely, God's love has been poured into our hearts through the Holy Spirit, and the fact of this generous outpouring is the basis for the apostle's assertion that hope does not disappoint us. Let us, with sure and certain hope, pour out our offerings before God, in love and with love, and so make our worship an imitation of Christ.

Prayer of Dedication

Triune God, with joy in your mighty acts of creation,
with gratitude for the peace that Jesus Christ has won for us,
with hope inspired by the Holy Spirit of truth and love,
we offer you these gifts;
may this outpouring of our thanksgiving be pleasing to you,
and productive in accordance with your will,
as a response to your continual blessing of your people
in this and every age.

The Charge and Blessing

Be bold to boast in your hope of glory,
trusting that hope will never disappoint,
for the one in whom you have placed your hope
is the holy, holy, holy God,
the Father, Son, and Holy Spirit,
who guides you and will bless you
as you go in the power of Jesus' name.

Proper 4
Ordinary Time 9 / May 29–June 4 (*if after Trinity*)

1 Kings 18:20–21 (22–29) 30–39
Psalm 96
Galatians 1:1–12
Luke 7:1–10

In Preparation for Worship

Lord God of our ancestors,
let it be known this day that you are God
in Israel, in the church, and over all things;
let it be known that I am your servant,
and that the whole gathered church is your priestly people.
Answer my prayer, O Lord; answer your people,
that those among whom we live in this land
may know that you alone, O Lord, are God,
and that you are turning their hearts to you
and to Jesus Christ your Son.

Call to Worship [Psalm 96]

Ascribe to the Lord, O families of the peoples,
ascribe to the Lord glory and strength.
> **Ascribe to the Lord the glory due his name;**
> **bring an offering, and come into his courts.**
Worship the Lord in holy splendor;
tremble before him, all the earth.

> Say among the nations, "The Lord is king!
> The world is firmly established; it shall never be moved.
> He will judge the peoples with equity."

Let the heavens be glad, and let the earth rejoice;
let the sea roar, and all that fills it;
let the field exult, and everything in it.

> Then shall all the trees of the forest
> sing for joy before the Lord; for he is coming,
> for he is coming to judge the earth.

God will judge the world with righteousness,
> and the peoples in truth.

Opening Prayer

Almighty God, your power is such that you need only speak the word and your sovereign authority is revealed. Yet your will is that we should have faith in you, trusting in you for all things, even when, by all accounts and outward appearances, we see little reason for faith. Draw near to us, O God, as we seek to draw near to you, that the altars of our hearts might be repaired, saturated with living water, and kindled anew by the fire of your Spirit, all for your glory and for the restoration of hope among your downcast people.

Call to Confession

The question that the prophet Elijah posed to the pagans in his day is just as pointed and pertinent in our own: "How long will you go on limping with two different opinions? If the Lord is God, follow him." Let us confess our sins to God!

Prayer of Confession

O Lord, God of Abraham, Isaac, and Israel, we confess we have grown so suspicious of authority that we have failed to recognize your own divine truth and power; we are often so self-concerned that we seek human approval rather than your own. Forgive us, O God, for misplacing our priorities, for cheapening and deserting your grace, and for confusing your gospel with the world's wisdom. Restore us to faith, in faith, and with faith, that we might even delight you with our faith, as did those rare saints who saw you in Christ Jesus and revered him as the one to whom all true authority has been given.

Declaration of Forgiveness

Friends, hear and believe the good news:
the Lord Jesus Christ gave himself for our sins
to set us free from the present evil age,
according to the will of our God and Father,
to whom be the glory forever and ever.
Neither is this gospel of human origin,
but it has come through a revelation of Jesus Christ,
in whom, through faith, you are forgiven.
Thanks be to God!

Presentation of Tithes and Offerings

God is a God who answers prayer, and does it in a way that reveals his divine authority in the sight of those who believe in him. This is why Jacob was named Israel, "one who sees God." Therefore, let us offer gifts to the Lord, that we might ask to see God's glory revealed according to the sovereign will of Christ for the upbuilding and instilling of faith in those who witness God's mighty and merciful acts in Jesus Christ.

Prayer of Dedication

Great are you, O Lord, and greatly to be praised.
Blessed be your holy name!
You are to be revered above all gods.
For all the gods of the peoples are idols,
but you have made the heavens.
Honor and majesty are due you;
strength and beauty are in your sanctuary.
Receive these gifts, O Lord,
as the singing of a new song,
as a witness to your salvation,
a declaration of your glory among all the nations.

The Charge and Blessing

The Lord answers, the Spirit reigns,
the promise of God is revealed in Jesus Christ!
Go forth from this place with single-minded devotion to the triune God,

trusting in God's soverign power to overcome the evils of this age,
and bearing witness to the life-giving and liberating gospel
of Jesus Christ our Lord.

Proper 5
Ordinary Time 10 / June 5–11 (*if after Trinity*)

1 Kings 17:8–16 (17–24)
Psalm 146
Galatians 1:11–24
Luke 7:11–17

In Preparation for Worship

O God, who reigns forever,
restore your Spirit in me today,
raise my hopes in eternity,
fill my heart as I use my voice
to offer songs and prayers of praise
raised from the depths of world-weariness,
up to you, Eternal God.

Call to Worship [Psalm 146]

Praise the Lord!
Praise the Lord, O my soul!
> I will praise the Lord as long as I live;
> I will sing praises to my God all my life long.

Happy are those whose help is the God of Jacob,
whose hope is in the Lord their God,
> who made heaven and earth,
> the sea, and all that is in them;
> who keeps faith forever.

The LORD will reign forever,
your God, O Zion, for all generations.
>   **Praise the LORD!**

Opening Prayer

Self-revealing God,
you have not left us alone to find our own way in the world,
but you have sent your Son to us, and given us your gospel truth.
Let not your Word be watered down by human wisdom,
but speak to us of holy things,
and bring us into the full knowledge
of your living grace in Jesus Christ.

Call to Confession

God is glorified when the wicked convert from sin to faith, when death gives way to new life. But who can convert or convince another apart from the grace of God and the gift of repentance? Therefore, do not put your trust in princes, in mortals, in whom there is no help. When their breath departs, they return to the earth; on that very day their plans perish. For God brings to ruin the way of the wicked, so that those who forsake their wicked ways may yet be saved. Let us confess our sin to God, turn anew from sin to Christ, and thus give glory to our gracious God.

Prayer of Confession

**God of Grace and Truth,
you have given us your law,
not for a weapon but for a guide.
Yet we, your church, have been either overzealous—
so eager for the law as to lose sight of the Spirit—
or too stubborn to submit.
Forgive us, O God, for our moralism and our permissiveness.
Help us trust you to command what is best
for us, for others, and for your kingdom,
where we are ever free to live in obedience to your holy will,
without fear of reprisal or condemnation.**

Declaration of Forgiveness

Hear the good news:
the Lord sets the prisoners free;
the Lord opens the eyes of the blind.
The Lord lifts up those who are bowed down;
the Lord loves the righteous,
those who live by faith in Jesus Christ, in whom we are forgiven.
Thanks be to God!

Presentation of Tithes and Offerings

The Lord upholds the orphan and the widow,
and watches over those who are strangers in the land.
God provides food for the hungry, and even brings the dead to life
for the sake of the lonely and bereaved.
What a compassionate and powerful God we serve!
Therefore, let us offer gifts to the one
who alone can restore life and hope
when he looks with favor upon his people.

Prayer of Dedication

Holy Lord, who opens the stores of heaven
for those on earth who trust in you,
speak your word of blessing over these humble provisions,
and multiply them as you desire,
that they may be used to feed the needy,
comfort the brokenhearted,
and fulfill every purpose to which you have assigned them;
this we ask in Jesus' name.

The Charge and Blessing

Go with the confidence that the Lord hears your prayers.
Go with the Word of Truth on your tongue.
Go with God's blessings, ready to bless,
in the name of Jesus Christ, our risen Lord.

Proper 6
Ordinary Time 11 / June 12–18 (*if after Trinity*)

1 Kings 21:1–10 (11–14) 15–21a
Psalm 5:1–8
Galatians 2:15–21
Luke 7:36—8:3

IN PREPARATION FOR WORSHIP

Lord Jesus,
you have forgiven me much,
indeed, far more than I know.
Bring your grace to my mind
that I may live and worship you in love and gratitude;
but let my mindfulness of your grace never be cause
to take back upon myself the guilt of my sins
or the weight of the law
or the burden of my justification.
Rather, let me live with and delight in you
as you live in and do your work through me,
for your good pleasure and glory.

CALL TO WORSHIP

Give ear to my words, O LORD;
give heed to my sighing.
> **Listen to the sound of my cry,**
> **my King and my God, for to you I pray.**
O LORD, in the morning you hear my voice;
in the morning I plead my case to you, and watch.

> I will enter your house
> through the abundance of your steadfast love.
>
> I will bow down toward your holy temple
> in awe of you.
>
> > Lead me, O LORD, in your righteousness
> > because of my enemies; make your way straight before me.

Opening Prayer

Redeeming God, what a wonderful new way of being is opened up to us through faith in Jesus Christ! For he alone is able to justify and reconcile us to you as we ourselves, striving to keep the law, never could. Come, we pray, and be present to us through Christ your living Word and through the gift of the Holy Spirit, whom you send in love, that we may worship you in love.

Call to Confession

Let us not think we can nullify the grace of God; for if we are justified through the law, then Christ died for nothing. But in fact, no one will be justified by the works of the law, for the law can only reveal our sinful nature. True justification comes by faith in Jesus Christ, faith not only professed, but lived by the power of the indwelling Christ. Let us confess our sins and our need for Christ to be formed within us.

Prayer of Confession

Holy God, you are not a God who delights in wickedness; evil will not sojourn with you. The boastful will not stand before your eyes, for you abhor the bloodthirsty and deceitful. We confess, O God, that though we profess faith in Jesus Christ, we have harbored envy and covetousness; we have justified ourselves by casting aspersions on others; we have done evil in your sight. Forgive us, O God, for our sins of mind and heart, body and will. Help us live by faith in the Son of God, considering ourselves crucified with Christ and dead to sin, that Christ Jesus might indeed live within each of us; for surely this is the very purpose for which he gave himself for us in love; thus, we ask your forgiveness and mercy in Jesus' name.

Declaration of Forgiveness

Hear the good news: though none of us can pay the debts we owe to our holy and righteous God, Christ our Redeemer has cancelled them by paying them for us. Not only this, but he has given us the gift of saving faith, and with it, himself, saying, "Your faith has saved you," for Christ Jesus himself is our faith. Therefore, make room for Christ in your hearts, abide with him, and be at peace.

Presentation of Tithes and Offerings

Scripture testifies that many whom Jesus cured of evil spirits and infirmities provided for his earthly ministry out of their own resources. Likewise, he revealed that those of whom much has been forgiven will be generous with works of love, outpourings of adoration, and offerings of hospitality. Let us likewise show our love to God in Christ through our tithes and offerings.

Prayer of Dedication

Mindful of your kindness, O God,
awed by the height and the depth of your love,
we offer you these gifts in the name of Jesus Christ,
whose offering on our behalf was perfect.
Regard with favor, we pray, these gifts,
that they may serve to exalt your holy name
and speak of the loving presence of Christ Jesus
in the midst of your church.

The Charge and Blessing

Go forth in the presence of Christ,
no longer directed, as you once were, by self-concern,
but with Christ the Lord alive in you
and leading you in his righteousness.
And may the Spirit of God anoint you,
the love of Christ fill you,
and the grace of God inspire
your every work and word.

Proper 7
Ordinary Time 12 / June 19–25 (*if after Trinity*)

1 Kings 19:1–4 (5–7) 8–15a

Psalms 42 AND 43

Galatians 3:23–29

Luke 8:26–39

In Preparation for Worship

O God, my God, my only hope,
I praise you again, my help and my God.
With the longing thirst of a deer
and a deadly wound in my body,
I thirst for you, O God,
my help and my God.

Call to Worship

Where there is love, discipline is not lacking.
> This is why God gave the law in love,
> that the children of God might know protection,
> discipline, and self-control.

Where there is faith, freedom is not lacking.
> But as we keep faith with Christ,
> we are free from the supervision of the law.
> As God's trusted children we take God's interests to heart.

Where Christ is, God's children are of one mind and purpose.
> All who belong to Christ
> are heirs of God's promise to Abraham.
> Let us worship our loving and generous God!

Opening Prayer

Send out your light and your truth, O God,
and guide us on your way.
Sustain us on our journey
and draw us into your holy presence,
that we might take refuge in you,
lifting up our songs and shouts of joy
in praise of your power and glory!

Call to Confession

Our Lord Jesus Christ, Son of the Most High God,
has healing and peace at his command.
Christ is good, far greater than every evil power,
and, with a word, will restore a right spirit within you.
So cast off the chains and bonds that bind you,
and place yourself at the feet of Christ in confession.

Prayer of Confession

**God of Peace,
we confess that our zeal for our own will
exceeds our zeal for yours.
We have confused your discipline with punishment,
your patience with approval,
your uncompromising desire for our well-being with severity.
Have mercy upon us, O Lord.
Show us into your holy will
and give us courage to embrace it
for the sake of Jesus Christ,
in whom we are one.**

Declaration of Forgiveness

Christ commands and the spirits obey.
Shall we respond with any lesser obedience
when the Lord of all creation forgives us and says,
"Let it be known how much God has done for you"?
Beloved in Christ, you are forgiven,
no longer chained as prisoners under the law,

but trusted to live responsibly, with joy and thanksgiving,
for you now belong to Christ,
heirs of all the promises that God has made
to the children of faith.

Presentation of Tithes and Offerings

As children of God we share a common heritage.
As heirs of the promise, we form a commonwealth.
As we belong to Christ, so let us share,
openly and with joy, what God has graciously given us.

Prayer of Dedication

Blessed God,
you have fed us in the wilderness,
watered us in the desert,
and preserved our lives from the wicked.
In the silence we tremble when we realize that,
without you, we have no life at all,
but with you, a great inheritance of faithfulness, fruitfulness, and freedom.
Therefore, we respond in this act of thanksgiving;
may it be a testimony to all that you have done for us
in Christ Jesus.

The Charge and Blessing

The Lord commands us to show mercy and steadfast love.
Live each day to fulfill this loving command.
The Spirit inspires within us songs of comfort and peace in the night.
Make each prayer a song to the Lord from the depths of your soul.
Christ leads us in a great procession to the kingdom of God.
Follow the light and the truth unfailing,
and praise the Lord daily with exceeding joy!

Proper 8
Ordinary Time 13 / June 26–July 2

2 Kings 2:1–2, 6–14
Psalm 77:1–2, 11–20
Galatians 5:1, 13–25
Luke 9:51–62

IN PREPARATION FOR WORSHIP

O God, who calls us onward and upward,
may we not forsake our calling to freedom,
or forget the mantel with which you have yoked us,
or feed the desires of the flesh.
But grow within us, and without us,
the fruits which bear witness to your Holy Spirit,
that our lives may be pleasing to you.

CALL TO WORSHIP

In the day of trouble, seek the LORD.
Cry out to God, and you will be heard.
> Let us meditate on the works of the LORD,
> and consider God's mighty deeds.

Your way, O God, is holy!
What god is so great as our God?
> You are the God who works wonders;
> you have displayed your might among the peoples!

Even the waters are afraid of you.
The very deep trembles at your awesome presence.

> You redeem your people with your strong arm,
> you lead your flock by the hand of the prophets,
> though you yourself are unseen.

When your souls refuse to be comforted, O people,
> then we will call to mind the deeds of the Lord!

Opening Prayer

God of freedom,
we come hoping to be guided by your Spirit,
so that we might find true freedom in you;
we come seeking to live by your Spirit,
so that we might bear good fruit for you.
May our choices ever bring us closer to you
and enrich your holy kingdom.

Call to Confession

Are you willing to be homeless, to forsake all that is familiar,
for the sake of the gospel, and never look back?
Are you fit for the kingdom of heaven?
Are you so full of the Holy Spirit
that you no longer want what you want at all,
but only what God desires?
If your heart does not belong perfectly, but only partially, to the Lord,
then let us join together in confessing our sins and shortcomings to God.

Prayer of Confession

Merciful God,
we confess we have used our freedom
for self-indulgence, competition, strife, and jealousy.
Our desires of the flesh have opposed your Spirit,
putting us at odds with one another and with you.
Forgive us, O God.
Take from us our lustful and vain desires;
nail them to the cross of our Lord Jesus Christ;
and set us free again to live by your Spirit,
that the fruits you find most pleasing
might be born in us today,
through Jesus Christ our Lord. Amen.

Declaration of Forgiveness

The God who desires our total obedience
and our undivided loyalty is the same God
who parts the waters that threaten to drown and destroy us.
Those who belong to Christ have crucified the flesh
with its passions and desires.
As you have been washed, raised, and now live by the Spirit,
so be guided by the Spirit, for in the Spirit of our Lord Jesus Christ,
you are no longer subject to the law,
but all your sins are forgiven.

Presentation of Tithes and Offerings

The whole law is summed up in a single commandment:
"You shall love your neighbor as yourself."
Therefore, let us love one another, not as pure emotion,
but in the concrete, material, physical act of sharing.
Such love for each other is pleasing to God,
the tangible testimony of our true love for God.

Prayer of Dedication

Remembering, O Lord, the mighty deeds and awesome wonders
you have performed on our behalf,
we offer you these gifts with gratitude and joy.
May the Spirit in which they are given be your Holy Spirit,
and the fruit they bear for the kingdom of Christ
be the fruit of holiness, grown in freedom.

The Charge and Blessing

Give the Holy Spirit freedom to use you,
and you will yield the fruit of the Spirit.
Give Jesus your total devotion and trust,
and in following Christ you will surely lead others.
Give God praise in all that you do,
and may the Creator of all things
guide you to your holy destination
in the kingdom of heaven.

Proper 9
Ordinary Time 14 / July 3–9

2 Kings 5:1–14

Psalm 30

Galatians 6:(1–6) 7–16

Luke 10:1–11, 16–20

In Preparation for Worship

I come with little, O God,
but the seeds you have given me to sow.
Let them be sown in the Spirit.
Let them produce a harvest
of peace and goodness,
to be gathered in for the good of all.

Call to Worship

Sing praises to the Lord, O people of faith!
Give thanks to the holy name of the Lord!
> **God's anger is but for a moment.**
> **But the favor of the Lord is for a lifetime!**

Weeping may linger for the night, but joy comes with the morning.
> **By your favor, make me a strong mountain,**
> **that I might never be moved.**

What profit is there in my death, if I go down to the Pit?
> **Will the dust praise you?**
> **Will it tell of your faithfulness?**

You have turned my mourning into dancing,
and clothed me with joy!
> **My soul will praise you and not be silent!**
> **O Lord, I will give thanks to you forever!**

Opening Prayer

Lord of the Harvest,
come and equip your laborers to be sent into your harvest,
to speak the gospel of peace to this troubled land,
to heal the sick and proclaim your kingdom,
that the power of the enemy might be broken,
and the names of all your servants might be written
in the kingdom of heaven.

Call to Confession

Bring to the Lord your brokenness and pain,
your sins and sorrows,
your despair and dismay.
God is gracious, and will exchange for them
healing, joy, and peace.
Let us humbly submit ourselves to God
for examination, repentance, and renewal,
confessing our sins.

Prayer of Confession

Healing God,
we admit that our expectations of you are often grand,
yet we fail to appreciate the grandeur of your simplicity.
We have yet to learn the great joy of humility,
and how pitiable are our claims and our clamourings
to be more than we are.
We have sinned. Cleanse us, O Lord.
Restore us gently, we pray,
to a right spirit and a right understanding
of the cost of discipleship
and the cross of our Lord Jesus Christ.

Declaration of Forgiveness

You have been crucified to the world of sin,
and the world is no longer for you.
But let your mourning be turned into dancing.
Let your hearts rejoice that you are free and freely forgiven.
For you are a new creation in Christ.
Boast no more of anything, except the cross of our Lord Jesus Christ.
Tell the world of all that God has done for you,
and may Christ's peace be upon you all.

Presentation of Tithes and Offerings [Galatians 6:7–8, 10]

Do not be deceived. God is not mocked, for you reap whatever you sow.
If you sow to your own flesh, you will reap corruption from the flesh;
but if you sow to the Spirit, you will reap eternal life from the Spirit.
Take every opportunity to work for the good of all,
and especially for those of the family of faith.
Let us sow the seeds of our tithes and offerings in the spirit of humility.

Prayer of Dedication

Gracious God, we cannot purchase our freedom.
We can only thank you for setting us free.
We cannot boast of our independence.
We can only praise you for being so dependable.
We cannot claim anything for ourselves.
We can only proclaim that your kingdom of love and mercy is at hand.
Therefore we thank you, praise you, and proclaim you Lord,
in the humble offering of these humble gifts.
Bless them and use them for your holy majesty.

The Charge and Blessing

The harvest is plentiful, but the laborers are few;
therefore, ask the Lord of the harvest
to send out laborers into the harvest.
Go on your way.
See, God is sending you out like lambs into the midst of wolves.
Whatever house you enter, first say, "Peace to this house!"
Whoever listens to you listens to Christ,

and whoever rejects you rejects the God who sends you.
Therefore, rejoice that your names are written in the kingdom of heaven!

Proper 10
Ordinary Time 15 / July 10–16

Amos 7:7–17
Psalm 82
Colossians 1:1–14
Luke 10:25–37

In Preparation for Worship

God of Justice, your standard is in our midst,
silently measuring our truth and our falsehood.
Refine us and build us into your own true temple,
that your high, holy place
might be filled with your praise.

Call to Worship

God is seated in the court of heaven.
The Lord judges all lesser gods, saying,
> "How long will you judge unjustly,
> and be partial to the wicked?
"Give justice to the weak and the orphan;
defend the right of the poor and lowly.
> "They have neither knowledge nor understanding,
> they walk around in darkness;
> the foundations of the earth are shaken.
"You are gods, children of the Most High, all of you!
Nevertheless, you shall die like mortals, and fall like any prince!"
> Rise up, O God, and judge the earth!
> For all the nations belong to you!

Opening Prayer

Redeeming God,
by whose grace men and women are prepared to share
in the inheritance of the saints in the light:
fill us with the knowledge of your will,
that we may live lives worthy of your name,
fully pleasing to you, as we seek to bear fruit in every good work
and grow in our knowledge of your Son Jesus Christ.

Call to Confession

We cannot comprehend the grace of God
until we first fathom our deep need for forgiveness,
and we cannot appreciate our need for forgiveness
until we first estimate the costliness of sin.
Sin takes hold when we wander from God.
But when we return to God in humility and faith,
we find Christ is able to rescue us from the power of darkness
and transfer us into the fellowship of believers
who dwell in the eternal light of heaven.
So let us all turn to God,
confessing our sins with the sure hope of forgiveness.

Prayer of Confession

**Our compassionate God,
we confess we have lost sight of our neighbors,
sought our own comforts,
and refused to be burdened
by the concrete demands of love.
We have even tried to justify ourselves before you,
the only true source of our justification.
Have mercy upon us, O Lord,
even as you revive in our hearts
the mercy you would have us show to this world,
so lost in darkness, so in need of love.
We ask this in Jesus' name.**

Declaration of Forgiveness

May your faith in Christ Jesus increase.
May your love for all the saints be multiplied.
May you know and be assured that there is a great store of hope in heaven,
laid up for you, that you may grow, be strengthened, and filled
with the spiritual wisdom and knowledge of God.
Be patient and joyful, therefore,
enduring everything and giving thanks
for your redemption in Jesus Christ.
God wills it! So let it be done.

Presentation of Tithes and Offerings

The gospel is bearing fruit throughout the world.
The word of truth is growing.
We are free to participate in that fruitfulness,
to contribute to its growth, or to deny and resist it.
Let us endeavor to please the Lord with every good work,
choosing the right, the loving, the compassionate,
and the generous way.

Prayer of Dedication

Eternal God, you have already given us a stake in your eternal kingdom.
What possible good can it do us to trust
in the things of this temporary world
or to attempt to withhold them from you?
Receive these gifts, given in joy.
May they join the ceaseless flow of holy blessings
by which your body is strengthened,
your people are nurtured,
your name is exalted,
and your will is done.

The Charge and Blessing

As God has been gracious to you, go and do likewise.
As Christ has shown compassion to you, go and do likewise.
As the Spirit stirs God's love within you,
go into the world and do likewise.

Proper 11
Ordinary Time 16 / July 17–23

Amos 8:1–12

Psalm 52

Colossians 1:15–28

Luke 10:38–42

IN PREPARATION FOR WORSHIP

We appear at your feet, O Christ,
weighed down with sins and sorrows,
bent down with broken hearts.
We kneel at your feet, O Savior,
stripped of all self-sufficiency,
awaiting your restoring word.

CALL TO WORSHIP

Why do the mighty boast of mischief done against the godly?
All day long they plot destruction, they lie, and act with treachery.
> **God will break down those who do evil!**
> **The Lord will snatch and tear them from their tents,**
> **and uproot them from the land of the living.**

The righteous will see it, and fear the Lord.
They will laugh at the evildoer and say,
> "See the one who would not take refuge in God,
> but trusted in abundant riches, and sought refuge in wealth!"

But I am like a green olive tree in the house of God.
I trust in the steadfast love of God forever and ever.

> I will thank you, O God, forever, for all you have done.
> In the presence of the faithful, I will attend to your good name.

Opening Prayer

We run to and fro, O Lord, seeking to hear a word from you.
We wander from sea to sea, O God, still we do not hear it.
Darkness covers the land, and our songs have turned to sorrow.
Break our fast with your words, and end the drought of your absence.
Come to us once again and speak, O God, for we your people are listening.

Call to Confession

Let all be warned. Let everyone be taught.
Let wisdom be heard and heeded by one and all.
Every believer shall be presented to God,
who desires our maturity in Christ.
Therefore, let every sin be confessed and renounced.
Let every distraction be stilled and silenced.
Let every deceit be exposed to the light of truth,
that your growth in Christ and Christ's growth in you
may resume and flourish with the hope of glory.

Prayer of Confession

God of Peace,
for all that we ever seek the right,
it seems we often choose the wrong.
We fail to see your fullness dwelling in our midst;
we fail to trust your power to save us;
we fail to live according to the peace
that you have made on our behalf
through the blood of your Son upon the cross.
Forgive us, O God, and help us choose the better way,
for the sake of Jesus Christ our Lord.

Declaration of Forgiveness

You who were once estranged and hostile in mind, doing evil deeds,
Christ has now reconciled in his fleshly body through his death,
so as to present you holy, blameless, and irreproachable before the Lord.

Therefore, stand secure and steadfast in the faith,
rooted in the hope promised you by the good news
that has been proclaimed to every creature under heaven.

Presentation of Tithes and Offerings

What shall we present to God through Christ,
who is before all things, firstborn of all creation,
through whom all things in heaven and earth were created?
In Christ the fullness of God is alive,
and we have partaken of this fullness!
Therefore, let us serve the Lord with what we have been given.

Prayer of Dedication

Reconciling God,
you have given us much to share from your fullness,
and you have given us many services to perform in your name.
As we set before you these resources for the ministry of your church,
we ask that your Holy Spirit would seal and consecrate them,
according to your will, and direct our work and our preparation
for the day when we too will be presented to you,
as the holy and mature work of Jesus Christ our Lord,
in whose name we pray.

The Charge and Blessing

The fullness of God is available in Jesus Christ.
Take part in God's fullness, as Christ grows in you.
Christ has made peace through his blood on the cross.
Be at peace with one another and with all creation, as the Spirit fills you.
For the Holy Spirit is the very source of your life, energy, and inspiration.
Stand firm, therefore, in the hope of glory,
as you work to make the word of God fully known.

Proper 12
Ordinary Time 17 / July 24–30

Hosea 1:2–10

Psalm 85

Colossians 2:6–15 (16–19)

Luke 11:1–13

In Preparation for Worship

Turn our hearts to you, O God, and attune all our senses.
Teach us to pray, that our prayers might be pleasing to you.
Let your words be heard among us, O God,
that your salvation might reach this troubled generation.

Call to Worship

People of God, the Lord invites you to a life of fullness,
rooted in Christ, established in faith.
> **We will not be deceived by human wisdom,**
> **but hold fast to Christ, who is our head.**

People of God, the Lord says, "Ask, and it shall be given.
Seek, and you will find. Knock, and the door will be opened."
> **We do not deny that this is God's way.**
> **Neither shall we doubt God's ability to answer prayer.**

People of God, put your trust in the Lord,
for he best knows what we truly need.
> **We praise you, O God, for your many good gifts!**
> **Fill us, we pray, with your Holy Spirit!**

Opening Prayer

Holy God,
who faithfully answers every prayer offered in true faith,
help us see the fullness that we have in Christ Jesus,
to rejoice in the nearness of your kingdom,
and to receive the growth that your Holy Spirit
inspires in us for your glory. Amen.

Call to Confession

The Lord gives what is good.
What the people need, God will not withhold.
Jesus Christ has taught us to ask,
with the added assurance that what we ask will be given.
Our Lord has instructed us to pray for forgiveness,
with the assumption that we ourselves have relinquished
all charges and accusations against our neighbors.
Let us do so, for such is the will of God.

Prayer of Confession

**You have been faithful, O God of mercy,
to forgive our former, and even our future, sins.
Yet we are slow to forgive the faults of others,
and slower still to admit and forgive our own.
Your loving faithfulness gives us reason to hope
that your anger and your indignation are but for a moment.
Therefore, revive and restore us again, O Lord.
Show us your steadfast love,
and grant us your salvation,
that we may rejoice in you.**

Declaration of Forgiveness

Steadfast love and faithfulness will meet;
righteousness and peace will come together.
Faithfulness will spring up from the ground,
and righteousness will look down from the sky.
God has made us alive together with Christ,
forgiving our sins and erasing the record

that stood against us with its accusations from the law.
God has set this aside, nailing it to the cross.
Therefore, as you have received Christ Jesus the Lord,
continue to live your lives in him,
rooted and built up in him and established in the faith,
just as you were taught,
abounding in thanksgiving!

Presentation of Tithes and Offerings

The glory of the Lord dwells in our land,
and the land has yielded its increase.
As we have received of God's rich fullness,
let us render our gifts for the work and ministry of Christ's church,
the body in which God's fullness dwells.

Prayer of Dedication

We thank you, Lord,
for the daily provisions with which you faithfully care for your creatures.
We praise you, O God, for your kingdom in which your holiness reigns.
We invite you, O Spirit, to come upon us and cleanse us,
even as you appropriate these gifts
and make them good according to your wisdom,
for the outworking of your will.

The Charge and Blessing

Ask, seek, knock—and it will be given, found, opened.
Even now, the door is flung wide,
and God imparts the fullness of divine blessings.
Therefore, receive the Holy Spirit,
grow with a growth that is from God,
and hold fast to Jesus Christ,
in whom you are rooted and established in faith.

Proper 13
Ordinary Time 18 / July 31–August 6

Hosea 11:1–11
Psalm 107:1–9, 43
Colossians 3:1–11
Luke 12:13–21

In Preparation for Worship
Eternal God,
we see how impoverished
our prosperity has left us.
Make us rich in you.

Call to Worship
Come, friends, and be gathered to the Lord.
Do not set your minds on earthly things.
>   **Let us seek the things that are above,**
>   **where our life is hidden with Christ in God!**

Come from east and west, from north and south.
Remember God's wonderful works to humankind.
>   **Let us give thanks to the Lord, for God is good.**
>   **The Lord is forever steadfast in love!**

Come, all you whom the Lord has redeemed.
For God satisfies the thirsty and fills the hungry with good things.
>   **Let us be wise and give heed to these things,**
>   **and consider the steadfast love of the Lord.**

OPENING PRAYER

Gracious God,
you are all in all!
Come and make us new,
according to your image,
and clothe us in Christ,
that when our Savior is revealed,
we may be revealed with him in glory.

CALL TO CONFESSION

Scripture testifies that the wrath of God is real,
and is coming upon those who are willfully disobedient.
Put to death, therefore, whatever in you is earthly,
impure, greedy, and idolatrous,
and confess it to the Lord.
Strip off the old self and its former ways.
Prepare to be created anew in confession,
according to God's perfect image,
as we see it, know it, and receive it in Christ Jesus.

PRAYER OF CONFESSION

**Loving God,
you have been to us like those who bend down to infants,
lift them up, and feed them.
You alone can teach us to walk aright;
you alone have been our source of strength and healing.
Yet we are a stubborn and forgetful people,
and we quickly turn away from you and go our own way.
Do not give us up, O Lord, or lift your hand of protection.
Forgive us and receive us as we humbly return to you.
This we ask in Jesus' name.**

DECLARATION OF FORGIVENESS

Our holy God, who is offended by sin,
is nevertheless, unlike mere mortals,
compassionate and tenderhearted toward sinners.
When God roars like a lion, sinners come trembling after,

and the LORD returns them to their homes.
Friends, God has delivered you from your distress.
Therefore, clothe yourselves in Christ,
and do not forget the steadfast love and mercy of God,
the mercy and grace through which we are saved
by Jesus Christ our Lord.

PRESENTATION OF TITHES AND OFFERINGS

The foolish hoard,
but those who are rich in God
seek the things that are above.
They share what they do not need,
they remember the goodness and mercy that God has shown them,
and they give thanks in everything.
We, who have been raised with Christ Jesus,
know the Lord is all in all.
Thus, we lack for nothing!
With gratitude, let us share God's plentiful blessings,
for it is in sharing that we are most richly blessed.

PRAYER OF DEDICATION

Giving and forgiving God,
you have given to us that we might share,
you have forgiven us that we might be a revelation
of your glorious new creation.
Make these earthly treasures
into heavenly testaments to your good news,
holy instruments of your good will,
harbingers of your good intentions
for the healing of this generation.
We ask this in Jesus' name.

THE CHARGE AND BLESSING

Do not stop the flow of God's blessings,
but direct them as the Spirit leads.
Do not stray from the ways of the Spirit,
but seek the things that are with Christ above.

Do not neglect your new life in Christ,
but be renewed by the image of your Creator,
and clothed with Christ who is all in all!

Proper 14
Ordinary Time 19 / August 7–13

Isaiah 1:1, 10–20

Psalm 50:1–8, 22–23

Hebrews 11:1–3, 8–16

Luke 12:32–40

In Preparation for Worship

We make ready, O Divine Master,
to receive you when you come.
As our treasure unfailing is with you,
so may our hearts be also.

Call to Worship

Those who bring thanksgiving as their sacrifice
show honor to the Lord as is right and just.
> **To those who choose the right way,**
> **God will grant eternal salvation.**

The mighty One, God the Lord, speaks and summons the earth
from the rising of the sun to its setting.
> **Our God comes and does not keep silence.**
> **The heavens declare the righteousness of the Lord,**
> **for God alone is judge.**

God says, "Gather around me, O my faithful ones,
all you who seek to live in covenant with me."
> **Let us attend to the Lord, with all creation,**
> **that God may render judgment in his gracious wisdom.**

Opening Prayer

Faithful God,
be not ashamed to be called our God,
for we seek you in faith and trust in your promise of a holy city,
of which you are the builder and Christ the sure foundation.
Grant us a vision of your better country, the heavenly homeland
that you have promised and prepared by your word.

Call to Confession

We know neither the day nor the hour
when Christ will come again for us.
Therefore, we must be ready at all times.
Let us seek the cleansing of forgiveness,
and the removal of all evil from our lives
by confessing our sin to God.

Prayer of Confession

Righteous God,
we confess that we have too often
sought treasure where it is not,
failed to do justice,
and ignored the social ills in which we participate.
Our sins are like scarlet and crimson before you.
Wash us clean, O God, and remove the stain of sin from our lives.
Awaken in us your own lasting goodness,
your desire for justice,
your living faith.

Declaration of Forgiveness

The Lord has spoken:
those who refuse the cleansing grace of God
and rebel against the Lord's commandments shall be devoured.
But not you who are willing to serve and obey the Lord.
You are cleansed of sin.
Remain awake and alert in Christ,
and you shall enjoy the good fruit of the land,

for the Lord will bless you.
Know that you are forgiven and be at peace.

Presentation of Tithes and Offerings

No thief can touch and no moth can destroy
the treasures we store up in heaven
by selling our possessions, giving alms,
and forsaking all we have left behind.
For if we are destined for heaven,
our hearts will be there long ahead of us,
and nothing on earth will ensnare us or weigh us down.
Thus free from the weight of earthly things
let us give thanks to the Lord.

Prayer of Dedication

Gracious God, our sacrifices are ever before you,
yet you desire no other sacrifice than our thanks,
no other offering than that we should choose the way of salvation
which is the great reward of faith.
In offering these treasures for your holy work,
we put the past behind us
and rededicate ourselves to following you
toward the home that you are preparing for us.
Accept these gifts and use them to refine your church in faith
and to make the world more fit to receive
the revelation of your holy word
as it has been spoken in Jesus Christ our Lord.

The Charge and Blessing

Be assured of the promise and keep faith in God,
for the Lord is busy preparing a new world.
Be dressed for action and keep your lamps lit,
for Christ will soon come to take you there.
Be hopeful and rich in the things of heaven,
and the Holy Spirit will furnish your eternal home.

Proper 15
Ordinary Time 20 / August 14–20

Isaiah 5:1–7

Psalm 80:1–2, 8–19

Hebrews 11:29—12:2

Luke 12:49–56

In Preparation for Worship

We look to you, Lord Jesus,
for you have endured the shame of the cross for us,
and you are now highly exalted.
Restore us and give us life, O Lord.
Let your face shine upon us,
that we may be saved.

Call to Worship

Turn again, O God of hosts,
look down from heaven and see;
> **regard this vine that you have planted,**
> **connected as we are to your chosen people.**

The church of this generation is laid waste,
the vine for which you cleared the ground!
> **Regard this church that you have planted,**
> **united as we are in the Lord Jesus Christ.**

Do not let your witnesses fall silent,
like a vineyard that is trampled and overgrown.
> **Regard this people of the faith you have nurtured,**
> **rooted as we are in your holy Word.**

Opening Prayer

We gather, O God, with your great cloud of witnesses,
whose reward is not separate from our own.
Help us persevere in the faith,
trust in your promises,
and hope in our Lord Jesus Christ,
who is risen and seated at your right hand in glory!

Call to Confession

"Since we are surrounded by so great a cloud of witnesses,
let us also lay aside every weight and the sin that clings so closely."
Let us accept the peace that God has made with us
through the blood of Jesus Christ,
and seek reconciliation with our neighbors while there is still time.
In good faith and humility, we confess our sins to God.

Prayer of Confession

**Loving and compassionate God,
we recognize that you have done everything needful for us
to lead holy and fruitful lives,
yet, where you expect justice, you see anger and violence;
where you expect righteousness, you hear of sin;
where you expect us to yield good fruit, we have gone sour.
Forgive us, O God.
Stir up your might, and come to save us!
Rescue us from ourselves
and separate us from sin.**

Declaration of Forgiveness

We have been given life
in order to call on the name of the Lord!
The God who led Israel out of Egypt
and freed his people from slavery
is the same God who loves us, disciplines us,
and restores us through Jesus Christ.
The world is not worthy of Christ,
who endured the cross to save the world from sin.

But have faith! Trust in the Lord!
As we are in Jesus Christ, we are set apart from the world;
we are forgiven and set free for new life.

Presentation of Tithes and Offerings

The God who establishes us in faith,
who nurtures and sustains us like a fruitful vineyard,
expects a good harvest.
May our giving be a testimony to our life in Christ,
a public demonstration that we share in the one faith
in the eternal God to whom our ancestors bore witness,
to whom we entrust our very lives.

Prayer of Dedication

Not only these tokens of our love, O Lord,
but our way of being in the world testify to our faith in you.
May we declare the greatness of your glory
by ever greater acts of faith,
with lives lived in trustful obedience,
hopeful integrity, and grateful stewardship.
May this act of sharing and the orientation of our hearts
be pleasing to you, and give you a joyful return, in Jesus' name.

The Charge and Blessing

Let us follow the Holy Spirit from this place,
and "run with perseverance the race that is set before us,
looking to Jesus the pioneer and perfecter of our faith,
who for the sake of the joy that was set before him,
endured the cross, disregarding its shame,
and has taken his seat at the right hand of the throne of God."
Trust in Christ, who perfects us with our ancestors, that,
through faith, we might receive with them the promised inheritance.
Go, therefore, and serve the Lord faithfully,
in this blessed assurance and peace.

Proper 16
Ordinary Time 21 / August 21–27

Jeremiah 1:4–10

Psalm 71:1–6

Hebrews 12:18–29

Luke 13:10–17

IN PREPARATION FOR WORSHIP

God of the Sabbath,
let your healing begin,
let your name be praised,
let your holy works be done this day.
Set us free from all that binds or weighs us down,
that we may stand upright
and praise your name!

CALL TO WORSHIP

The Lord has promised to shake the earth and the heavens once more.
God's voice shakes the earth and all created things.
> **Yet God gives us a kingdom that cannot be shaken.**
> **The LORD alone is our fortress and refuge.**

Give thanks to God, a consuming fire.
Worship the Lord with reverence and with awe!
> **God has been our hope and our trust.**
> **We shall forever praise the LORD.**

Come then to Zion, to the city of the living God.
Come to Jesus in the heavenly Jerusalem.

If we do not refuse the One who is speaking,
the LORD shall enroll us in the assembly of heaven!

Opening Prayer

Healing God,
we gather in anticipation of your eternal Sabbath,
when all who are afflicted will finally be healed,
and all who are oppressed will be set free.
Incline your ear to save us, O God.
In your righteousness, deliver and rescue us;
for those who worship you in spirit and in truth
will never be put to shame.

Call to Confession

The holy work of healing is fit for the Sabbath.
As Jesus cured on the Sabbath day,
so we should not hesitate to ask to be freed
from all that binds and troubles us.
In confession, let us ask our Lord Jesus Christ
to mend us in our broken places
and to make us fit for rendering
acceptable worship and grateful praise to God.

Prayer of Confession

**O God, who gave us birth and knew us before our beginnings,
we confess that in our timidity we miss your intention for us,
and we often fail to trust you to do something through us,
something greater than ourselves, greater than we can imagine.
Forgive us for our failures of faith.
Put your Word in our hearts and in our mouths,
that we might follow you more faithfully,
testify to you more powerfully,
and realize our divinely appointed end and purpose.**

Declaration of Forgiveness

God has promised to so shake heaven and earth,
until the only thing remaining will be the holy kingdom of Christ.

Therefore, be established in Christ
who is your rock and your fortress,
and seek the kingdom with gladness.
For those who trust in the mercy of the Lord
will never be put to shame.

Presentation of Tithes and Offerings

The gifts we give are but a visible sign
of our gratitude and our calling
to do the work God has appointed us to do
and to speak the words God has appointed us to speak.
Let us rededicate ourselves to sacred works and sacred speech
as we offer our gifts and our lives to God.

Prayer of Dedication

We praise you, Blessed God,
for including us in your plan
to purify and prepare a kingdom for your people,
and to build and to plant that kingdom in our midst.
May these gifts be used at your direction
to establish your kingdom that cannot be shaken.

The Charge and Blessing

As God has consecrated you by the Holy Spirit
to do good works,
to speak the truth,
and to live in hope of the coming kingdom,
go and show Christ's life to the world
in your life, in your labor, in your witness.

Proper 17
Ordinary Time 22 / August 28–September 3

Jeremiah 2:4–13

Psalm 81:1, 10–16

Hebrews 13:1–8, 15–16

Luke 14:1, 7–14

In Preparation for Worship

Our Lord Jesus Christ,
you are the same yesterday and today and forever!
Attend our humble gathering,
for we seek to be hospitable people,
welcoming your Word and
open to your Spirit.

Call to Worship

The Lord is our helper. We shall not be afraid.
No suffering or sadness can compare with the grace of God.
> **Let us give praise to God through Christ,**
> **confessing the name of Jesus.**

The Lord is our helper. We shall not be afraid.
For God has said, "I will never leave you or forsake you."
> **Let us be content with what God has given us,**
> **remembering those who suffer for the faith.**

The Lord is our helper. We shall not be afraid.
Indeed, God's angels are in our midst.
> **Let us not fail to show hospitality to strangers,**
> **loving one another with the love of Christ.**

Opening Prayer

God of Glory,
we seek you in the heights of heaven,
yet you are always with us
as we walk our humble, earthly way.
We look for you among the strong,
yet you confound us by appearing among the weak and the vulnerable,
the poor and the lame, the downtrodden and the downcast.
Give us your vision to see the dignity
of those we might ignore, to love as you do,
and to serve as those who bear the name of Christ.

Call to Confession

Let not your hearts be stubborn.
Let no one forsake the Lord.
For all who exalt themselves will be humbled,
and those who humble themselves will be exalted.
Let us remember and confess in humility
our sins against one another and against the Lord.

Prayer of Confession

**Gracious God,
we confess that we have pursued worthless things,
forsaking your fountain of living water
for cracked cisterns that can hold nothing.
We have been quick to affirm ourselves, and slow to honor others.
Forgive us, O Lord, and return us to the glory of your salvation,
in which all your children are valued, honored, and loved.**

Declaration of Forgiveness

Those who listen to the voice of the Lord
will be preserved and their enemies quickly subdued.
Those who walk in the ways of truth
will be fed with the finest of wheat,
with honey from the rock they will be satisfied.
Sing aloud to God our strength,
and shout for joy to the God of Jacob,

for forgiveness in Christ is sweet
for all who trust in God's mercy and grace.

Presentation of Tithes and Offerings

Scripture tells us: Keep your lives free from the love of money,
and be content with what you have; for God has said,
"I will never leave you or forsake you."
Through Christ, then, let us continually offer
a sacrifice of praise to God, that is,
the fruit of lips that confess the name of Jesus.
Do not neglect to do good and to share what you have,
for such sacrifices are pleasing to God.

Prayer of Dedication

We praise you, O Christ,
for your mercy leads us into love.
We bless you, loving Father,
for your voice calls us into the blessed way.
We thank you, Holy Spirit,
for you have guided, guarded, and gifted us beyond measure.
Thus, we would honor you, Holy God,
in our humble act of giving.

The Charge and Blessing

Let love continue and increase among you.
Let hospitality and compassion be shown.
Let humility be your rule for living,
and the triune God who creates, forgives, and inspires you
will bear you along to your eternal home.

Proper 18
Ordinary Time 23 / September 4–10

Jeremiah 18:1–11

Psalm 139:1–6, 13–18

Philemon 1–21

Luke 14:25–33

IN PREPARATION FOR WORSHIP

Creator God,
you know us intimately, mold us carefully,
and create us for a holy purpose.
Shape us deeply and fill us with your Spirit,
that we may each take the form you intend.

CALL TO WORSHIP

Come, O Lord, and regard your people.
For nothing is hidden from you, whose works are wondrous.
> Before a word is spoken, before a thought is fully formed,
> God knows it completely.

Come, O Lord, and search your people.
For you form each of us according to your design.
> How weighty are your thoughts, O God.
> How vast is the sum of them!

Come, O Lord, and set your people free.
Indeed, you have come, for you were here long before the ages began.
> We praise you, O God, for you are still with us.
> Lead us and show us the way to eternal freedom with you.

Opening Prayer

Holy and eternal God,
you are free to fashion us for your pleasure,
as a potter fashions clay into something beautiful and useful.
Make of us what you desire, that we might know freedom in service,
and joy in conforming to your perfect will.

Call to Confession

Nothing can be hidden from God,
for no darkness can overcome the light of the Lord.
No thought or motive can be kept from the Lord,
for God knows our thoughts from far away.
No one can truly flee from God,
for wherever we go God is already there.
Such is the constancy and faithfulness of our inescapable God!
Therefore, let us turn, one and all, from every evil way
and amend our ways and our doings.
We have no recourse but to confess our sins.

Prayer of Confession

**Our Lord Jesus Christ, crucified and risen,
you have called us to a journey of joyful service and freedom,
yet we remain tied to many things.
We fear the cost of discipleship
and forget the greater cost of fear.
We know to resist the sin of slavery,
yet we attach ourselves to people, to places, and to property
and find ourselves overwhelmed and mastered by them.
Forgive us, free us, and inspire us to faith,
that in our following you,
your kingdom of truth and love might be made
ever more visible to this world.**

Declaration of Forgiveness

Justice is seen only where God is revered, trusted, and loved.
Yet any true or thoughtful encounter that would result in such justice
must profoundly change us and reform our priorities

as we walk our earthly way.
The freedom that Christ has purchased for us is open to all his chosen;
yet many do not yet know and have not accepted the grace of Christ.
Let us not hide the good news from those who are lost and perishing.
But let us share it and shout it to the world.
In Jesus Christ, we are forgiven!

Presentation of Tithes and Offerings

In Christ, our bondage to objects is ended,
our oppressive ties to idols are cut.
Since we no longer serve any god but God,
let us demonstrate an uncompromising loyalty
by directing our resources, our energies, our lives, and our love
as the Holy Spirit inspires and leads.

Prayer of Dedication

Let nothing come between us, O God,
no material or spiritual or emotional tie.
Let no doubt dissuade us, let no fear restrain us
from giving you our undivided loyalty and love.
As you have given Christ Jesus to us,
we need no further assurance of your good will.
Receive then these gifts in witness to our faith,
and use them to draw more followers into your holy fellowship.

The Charge and Blessing

Let the Lord mold you into a vessel for the Spirit.
Let the Spirit fill you with the love of Christ.
Let Christ lead you into perfect freedom,
that your life may be a journey of true faith.

Proper 19
Ordinary Time 24 / September 11–17

Jeremiah 4:11–12, 22–28

Psalm 14

1 Timothy 1:12–17

Luke 15:1–10

In Preparation for Worship

In the barren wastes
into which we have wandered,
we turn and long for you to come.
From the dark corners into which we have strayed,
we watch for your searching light.
Seek and save us, O Great Shepherd,
and restore to us the joy
of your salvation!

Call to Worship

The Lord looks down from heaven:
are there any who are wise, who seek after God?
> **Everywhere fools say, "There is no God."**
> **Even the believers have wandered away!**

The earth is a waste, the heavens are dark.
The farms are a desert, and the cities are ruined.
> **The whole land shall become a desolation,**
> **yet God will not make a full end!**

Rejoice in the LORD, who rejoices over us
when we repent and renounce our wicked ways.
> **For there is more joy in heaven over those who repent
> than over those who need no repentance!**

OPENING PRAYER

Immortal, invisible God of the ages,
who welcomes sinners and eats with them,
who seeks and saves the lost, and who celebrates their salvation:
We thank you that, in your faithfulness and love,
you go to such extremes to find us,
and show such extravagance to your wayward sheep.
May all honor and glory be yours forever!

CALL TO CONFESSION

All alike have gone astray.
There is no one who does good—
no, not even one.
The deeds of human beings are corrupt at every level.
O that deliverance would come.
Yet it cannot come from human efforts.
It can only come from God.
What can sinners be thinking
who fail to call upon the Lord for mercy?

PRAYER OF CONFESSION

**We confess, O God,
that we have often thought, spoken, and acted
in ignorance and bad faith.
We have wandered from your flock, tested your patience,
and caused you grief by our many sins
against you and against one another.
Yet you, O God, are diligent in seeking us, untiring in your patience,
and quick to show your long-suffering compassion and mercy.
Gather us in once again, O God,
that the joy of heaven might be complete.**

Declaration of Forgiveness

The grace of our Lord overflows with the faith and the love
that are in Christ Jesus, who came into the world to save sinners.
Therefore, trust and accept this gospel news,
and believe in Jesus Christ for eternal life.

Presentation of Tithes and Offerings

Even though we may be foolish and prodigal
and do not know how to do good,
the Lord is with the company of the righteous;
and when the Lord restores the fortunes of his people,
there is always gladness and rejoicing.
Therefore, with trust and thanksgiving,
let us offer our gifts to God.

Prayer of Dedication

Thanks be to you, O Christ,
that you strengthen us and make us fruitful, despite our past sins;
you call us into service, despite our contrary ways.
As recipients of your grace, make us exemplary witnesses
in whom others may see your faith and love at work.
Receive and bless this offering,
that it may be used according to your will
and for the honor and glory of your name.

The Charge and Blessing

Seek the Lord in all that you do
and the Lord himself will reward you.
The Lord will reward you with himself!

Proper 20
Ordinary Time 25 / September 18–24

Jeremiah 8:18—9:1

Psalm 79:1–9

1 Timothy 2:1–7

Luke 16:1–13

In Preparation for Worship

Almighty God,
you are the source of our lives and our living,
you are the inspiration of our love and our giving.
Make us a channel for your blessings,
that your bounty might be shared with those indebted
and that we, your unworthy servants,
might be joyfully welcomed
into your eternal home.

Call to Worship

The Lord suffers the people's pain.
God is not above our mourning and dismay.
> **The harvest is past, and the summer is ended.**
> **Salvation tarries, and the poor cry out.**

The heart of the Lord is sick of corruption.
God is grieved by our idolatry.
> **Is there no physician, no balm in Gilead?**
> **Then why have the people not been healed?**

The Lord desires that all people should be saved.
God summons everyone to know the truth.
> Come to the Lord, O people of the earth.
> Offer up your prayers and declare God's worth.

Opening Prayer

Almighty God,
you have created all from nothing,
blessed us with everything,
and called us to practice the grateful stewardship of sharing.
Hear our songs in praise of your goodness.
Heed our cries for healing and wholeness.
Answer our pleas that your Spirit would come.

Call to Confession

There is only one God,
and there is only one mediator between God and humankind,
Christ Jesus, fully human, fully God,
who gave himself as a ransom for all.
Therefore, let us appeal for mercy
to Almighty God through Christ Jesus,
for the compassion of the God of our salvation
comes swiftly to those who are humble and lowly,
and who place their trust in the name of the Lord.

Prayer of Confession

**Giving and forgiving God,
you have made us a gifted people
and established us in a land of plenty.
We confess that we have forgotten
that all our material gifts are temporary,
and that you expect us to render an accounting.
Awaken us again to our sacred duties.
Make us aware of your continual grace.
Forgive us for every sin committed
and every missed opportunity
to obey the gospel.**

Declaration of Forgiveness

Indeed, there is a balm in Gilead,
a healing God who weeps for human sin,
whose head is a spring of living water.
The sins of the people are washed away,
but at a great price: the death of Christ Jesus,
who has purchased our freedom.
Let us then live lives of godliness and dignity,
of peace and grace, of truthfulness and prayer,
for such living is right
and acceptable in the sight of God.

Presentation of Tithes and Offerings

No slave can serve two masters;
for a slave will either hate the one and love the other,
or be devoted to the one and despise the other.
You cannot serve God and wealth.
Therefore, let us serve God by means of our wealth,
along with every other blessing that we have from the Lord.

Prayer of Dedication

Giver of all good gifts,
we seek to be good stewards
of everything you have given us
to administer in your name.
Guide us clearly with your Spirit of truth;
keep us faithfully within your holy will;
give us energy, that by the use of these, your instruments,
we might glorify the name of Jesus Christ our Lord.

The Charge and Blessing

Do not wait till the last minute
to be generous with God's gifts.
Do not postpone praying in the Spirit
for all those in authority.
Do not delay to tell the world the truth
about the great and loving gift of Jesus Christ.

Do it today and every day,
as the triune God inspires you.
Go in the name of Christ
and the power of the Spirit.

Proper 21
Ordinary Time 26 / September 25–October 1

Jeremiah 32:1–3a, 6–15

Psalm 91:1–6, 14–16

1 Timothy 6:6–19

Luke 16:19–31

In Preparation for Worship

Our Lord Jesus Christ,
our blessed and only Sovereign,
King of kings and Lord of lords,
we long to see you revealed to the world;
we invite your fullness to be formed within us;
so we offer ourselves to you.

Call to Worship

Let all who live in the shelter of the Most High God,
who abide in the shadow of the Almighty, say to the Lord,
> **"My refuge and my fortress,
> my God, in whom I trust!"**

For God will deliver you from the snare of the evil one;
the Lord will faithfully keep you from harm.
> **We will not fear the terror of the night,
> or the arrow that flies by day.**

God has declared, "Those who love me, I will deliver.
I will protect those who know my name, and answer them when they call.
> **"I will be with them in trouble, and rescue and honor them!
> I will satisfy them with long life, and show them my salvation!"**

Opening Prayer

Almighty God,
who alone is immortal and dwells in unapproachable light,
we seek you in order that we may take hold of eternal life,
the life in the Holy Spirit to which you have called us
and for which we publicly confess
our trust in the living Lord Jesus Christ.
All honor, glory, and dominion are yours,
triune God, forever and ever.

Call to Confession

God has promised to be with us in trouble,
to protect and provide for us.
In return, we offer our humble trust.
But such trust is empty without our willingness
to abandon our old, wasteful ways
and to adopt God's commandments as our rules for living.
This is repentance, the true measure of our faith in God.
Therefore, let us repent and turn to God,
confessing our sins and submitting ourselves
to the righteousness of the Lord.

Prayer of Confession

**God of justice and mercy,
who preserves the weak and protects the poor,
we confess that our selfish sins have hardened our hearts,
clouded our vision,
and made us slow to recognize and respond
to the pain, the vulnerability, and the value of others.
Forgive us, O Lord.
Protect us when we are tempted,
strengthen us to fight the good fight,
and inspire us to pursue
righteousness, godliness, faith,
love, endurance, and gentleness,
for your name's sake.**

Declaration of Forgiveness

The Lord's condemnation of sin is uncompromising.
We are to hate sin no less than we love the Lord!
But the Lord's love of sinners is also unmatched.
We are to strive for godliness and take hold of the eternal life
to which God has called us,
for which we have made the good confession
in the presence of many witnesses.
Now let us aspire to keep the commands of God blamelessly,
until our Lord Jesus Christ comes again,
in whom we are forgiven.

Presentation of Tithes and Offerings

There is much to gain
by living in godliness combined with contentment;
for we have brought nothing into the world,
and we can take nothing out of it.

Prayer of Dedication

God of Grace,
we seek contentment with what we have,
and we hope to ease the sufferings of others,
to participate in your wonderful work in the world.
Thus, we present these material gifts for your spiritual blessing,
that you might make them holy
and use them according to your will to love
and your love of mercy.
May you do the same with us,
for the love of Jesus.

The Charge and Blessing

Go forth to show the compassion of the Lord.
Be merciful to the suffering.
Be generous to the poor.
Search out the lost
and ask the Lord Jesus for redemption.
And may the righteousness of God,

the godliness of Christ,
and the faith and love of the Holy Spirit
make you content in everything
and keep you in eternal life.

Proper 22
Ordinary Time 27 / October 2–8

Lamentations 1:1–6

Lamentations 3:19–26 or Psalm 137

2 Timothy 1:1–14

Luke 17:5–10

IN PREPARATION FOR WORSHIP

Your people wait quietly for your salvation, O Lord,
though many are afflicted, homeless, and ground down by despair.
We wait, for you are good to those who wait on you.
Your steadfast love never ceases.
Therefore, our hope will ever be in you.

CALL TO WORSHIP

How can we sing the LORD's song in a foreign land?
What reasons have we for joy as we sojourn through a fallen world?
> **Forget not Jerusalem.**
> **Let us set it above our highest joy!**

Does not the holy city lie in ruins?
How empty and lonely she has become!
> **But the mercy of the LORD never ceases.**
> **God's love never ends.**

Indeed, the Lord did not give us a spirit of cowardice,
but his own Spirit of power to accomplish all things.
> **Let us wait for the LORD as humble servants do,**
> **for the Holy Spirit living within us is our eternal treasure,**
> **and by the Spirit the LORD will surely raise us up!**

Opening Prayer

Saving God,
who has brought life and immortality to light through the gospel,
we give you thanks for the fellowship we have with one another,
and with all your people, in the one body of our Lord Jesus Christ.
Strengthen us with sound teaching,
feed us by your word,
rekindle within us the gift of your Holy Spirit,
that we might serve you as we ought,
in love, in power, and in self-discipline.

Call to Confession

With just the smallest amount of faith,
even as small as a mustard seed,
great things like trees and mountains can be removed.
With the faith we have been given,
and in the spirit of penitence,
let us seek Christ in confession
and ask for the weight of sin to be removed.

Prayer of Confession

**Suffering God,
we confess that we have not understood
or practiced your holy ways;
we give in to fear,
shrink from costly commitments,
and seek our own comfort and leisure
as if deaf to your command.
Forgive us, refresh us, embolden us, and redirect us,
that we might serve you,
ever true to the faith and the love
that are in Christ Jesus.**

Declaration of Forgiveness

Believe the good news!
God has saved us and called us with a holy calling,
not according to our works

but according to the Lord's own holy purpose and grace.
This grace was given to us in Christ Jesus before the world began,
but now it has been revealed in our Savior Christ Jesus,
who has abolished death and brought life and immortality to light.
Know that, in Christ, we have new life!

Presentation of Tithes and Offerings

How shall we show our true obedience to God,
if we do not place ourselves at the disposal of God's Spirit?
How shall we fulfill our call to humble service,
if we do not submit our resources to the servant Lord who is our Master?
How shall we live in faith,
if we do not see our property as first belonging to God
by whose grace we have received it?

Prayer of Dedication

Fashion us, O God,
in the image of your servant,
and re-create us with the free flow of your blessing;
free us, O Christ, from the fetters of this world,
and redeem our spirits with this mutual outpouring;
fill us, O Spirit, with the joy of giving,
and refresh your creation through these gifts.

The Charge and Blessing

Be not ashamed of the gospel of our Lord,
but proclaim it boldly in word and deed.
Be not afraid of the costs of Christian service,
for your good treasure is guarded for you
with the help of the Holy Spirit.
Be not dismayed when suffering for the faith,
for the power of God will prosper and sustain you.

Proper 23
Ordinary Time 28 / October 9–15

Jeremiah 29:1, 4–7

Psalm 66:1–12

2 Timothy 2:8–15

Luke 17:11–19

In Preparation for Worship

Son of David, risen from the dead,
let your word be loosed among us,
that we may rightly understand your gospel truth
and proclaim it to others for their salvation.

Call to Worship

Present yourselves before the Lord
as those whom God has approved.
> **We are not ashamed of the gospel of our Lord Jesus Christ,**
> **neither shall we fear suffering for it.**

The apostles were chained and the prophets exiled,
but the word of the Lord is not chained and shall not return empty.
> **Let us build and plant and increase in the land.**
> **We will pray for the welfare of the church in the world.**

Bless the Lord, O people; lift up your praises in song,
for the Lord has kept us and established us in faith.
> **Let us sing to the glory of God.**
> **Let all the earth worship the Lord!**

Opening Prayer

Living God,
may all selfish concerns be put to rest,
that we may ever live for you;
may our faith in you endure all things,
that we may ever reign with you;
may we boldly proclaim your holy name,
that we may ever testify to you;
for your faith is perfect when ours is not,
indeed, you are always true.

Call to Confession

Those who cry out to Christ for mercy
the right hand of the Lord will save.
For the God who led Israel across the sea on dry land,
and preserved the people while in exile,
is the same God whose power is present in Jesus,
who heals the diseased and raises the dead.
Let us confess our sin to the God of mercy.

Prayer of Confession

We confess, Healing God,
that we are eager to receive but slow to return thanks,
long on despair and short on hope,
and all too easily misled by false teachings and empty thoughts.
We have passed some tests but failed many others.
Forgive us, restore us, and preserve us, O God.
Establish us in your will,
that the sound of your praise
might be heard among us.

Declaration of Forgiveness

Those who praise the Lord will be saved,
and their faith will make them well.
Those who remember God's awesome deeds
the Lord will keep from falling.
May you endure in your faith

in the mercy of the Almighty,
obtain salvation in Christ Jesus our Lord,
and attain the eternal glory.
Trust in the Lord,
and do not doubt God's forgiveness
and good will toward you.

Presentation of Tithes and Offerings

What does the Lord expect of those who are saved?
Thanksgiving, humility, and obedience.
When we honor God with our praise,
we open ourselves to a deeper form of healing,
and we are free to receive the grace that is ours
whenever we worship God with our whole being.
Let us show our faith in the trustful,
worshipful act of offering our gifts to God.

Prayer of Dedication

We praise you, O God,
remembering your mighty deeds
by which you delivered our ancestors, and us as well.
We thank you, O God, for the healing you have given us
by the power of the Holy Spirit.
We love you, O God, for the gift of salvation
that you have made possible in the suffering and bleeding,
the dying and rising of our Lord Jesus Christ.
May these humble gifts be expressions
of our heartfelt praise and thanks and love.

The Charge and Blessing

Remember Jesus Christ, who was perfectly obedient to God,
crucified, buried, and raised from the dead. That is the gospel!
Wherever you see suffering, whenever death threatens,
take courage in your God and serve one another in love.
Endure everything for the sake of your sisters and brothers in Christ,
who are chosen by God to receive salvation.
And may you ever live in the warmth and peace
of Christ's eternal glory!

Proper 24
Ordinary Time 29 / October 16–22

Jeremiah 31:27–34

Psalm 119:97–104

2 Timothy 3:14—4:5

Luke 18:1–8

In Preparation for Worship

We surrender our hearts to you,
that you may write your word upon them;
we draw our breath from you
to receive your inspiration.
In the presence of your Word, O Lord,
make us faithful, steadfast, and true.

Call to Worship

Keep covenant with the Lord.
Do not doubt God's abiding presence.
> The sacred writings point the way to salvation.
> Let us grow up with the Scriptures, as little children do.

Open your hearts to the word of the Lord.
Meditate on it day and night.
> The word of the Lord is sweet to the taste.
> Let us keep it by turning from every evil way.

Keep faith in the Lord.
Pray at all times, and do not lose heart.
> The Lord will grant our petitions quickly.
> Let us direct our concerns to our righteous God.

Opening Prayer

Merciful God, you are the only truly righteous judge,
eager to answer our prayers and pleas.
Your answer is swift and your words are true.
We gather to hear your word to us, making ready to be convicted,
hoping to be instructed, expecting to be energized,
that we may fully carry out your will.

Call to Confession

Sin is deadly and affects us all.
The Lord watches over us
and is determined to pluck up and remove
every evil seed that takes root in our lives.
Therefore, let us submit ourselves to God's examination and discipline,
so that the work of planting good seed might begin anew.
Let us confess our sins and receive God's merciful judgment,
which is only ever—truly!—for our own good.

Prayer of Confession

God of wisdom,
we admit that we have been slow
to reprove, correct, and train one another
in the ways of righteousness.
We have neglected the work of spreading the good news.
We lack confidence in our knowledge of Scripture,
and we fear offending others by coming on too strong.
Have mercy on us for our timidity and confusion.
Have mercy and fill us with love for all,
and for all that you reveal in your Word.

Declaration of Forgiveness

In Christ, God has promised a new covenant,
under which our iniquity is forgiven and our sin is remembered no more.
So let the law of the Lord be in you;
let the word of God be written on your contrite hearts.
Know the Lord for yourselves, each of you,
from the least to the greatest,

and trust the Lord for the mercy, correction, and instruction
that open, reveal, and give shape to your future life.

Presentation of Tithes and Offerings

God has shown us the way to live profitable lives:
guided by Scripture, taught by the Spirit,
and equipped in Christ for every good work.
We give generously because we have seen and known for ourselves
how generous the Lord has been to us,
providing all that we need and more.
Let us join the current of God's blessings,
by offering for God's use the gifts we have from above.

Prayer of Dedication

We seek to be free, O gracious God,
of self-serving doctrines and desires.
Thus, we lay these treasures at your feet,
that you might use them more perfectly than we can on our own.
We offer them to you, that others might enjoy
the fruits of your swift justice.
We take leave of them, trusting that your Spirit would direct them
to the places and uses where love can best take root
and grow and give you glory, in Jesus' name.

The Charge and Blessing

Let your hearts be filled with love for God's word.
Let your minds dwell in the Spirit of truth.
Let your souls be humble in Christlike obedience,
as you devote your bodies
in humble service to the kingdom of God.

Proper 25
Ordinary Time 30 / October 23–29

Joel 2:23–32
Psalm 65
2 Timothy 4:6–8, 16–18
Luke 18:9–14

In Preparation for Worship

Awesome God,
you have dealt wondrously with us in the past,
granting us plenty and abundance to fulfill all our needs.
Now pour out your Spirit on all human flesh.
Inspire us with dreams and visions
of truth and goodness, justice and peace,
that the world might finally know you are God.

Call to Worship

You are worthy of praise, O God, O you who answer prayer.
All creatures shall know your awesome presence.
> Happy are those whom you call, mighty God.
> When sin overwhelms us, you forgive and rescue us.

Let sinners repent and be made righteous in Christ.
The Lord is gracious in blessing his creation.
> We shall be satisfied with your goodness, O Lord,
> for you are the hope of all the earth.
> Let the morning and the evening shout for joy!

Opening Prayer

God of grace and mercy,
who justifies sinners and humbles all who exalt themselves,
we approach you meekly,
remembering the repentant tax collector who stood far off,
who would not even look up to heaven,
who was grieved by his sin,
and went home justified.
It is only by your grace
that we assemble in your name.

Call to Confession

God responds to our emptiness
by filling us and washing over us
with deep and powerful and cleansing grace.
The Lord will rescue us from every evil,
and from the overwhelming tide of sins
that threaten to undo us.
God will justify, save, and even bless us
when we pour out in confession
all that we have done to keep God at bay.
Therefore, keep nothing from God,
but rather be humble and lowly, and confess your sin.

Prayer of Confession

**Loving God,
we confess that we have been closed to the gift of your Holy Spirit,
blind to the visions with which you would bless us,
and afraid of the dreams you reveal to us.
We are tense, anxious, and distrustful.
Give us courage to trust you,
joy in receiving you,
and peace in relinquishing all our fears.
Pour out your Spirit upon us anew,
cleanse and inspire us,
for we call upon your holy name.**

Declaration of Forgiveness

Scripture says that all who call upon the name of the Lord will be saved.
O children of God, be glad and rejoice in the Lord your God,
who has dealt wondrously with you, saying,
"My people will never be put to shame."
Indeed, there is a crown of righteousness reserved for everyone
who has longed for the Lord's appearing;
keep faith in God, and Jesus Christ himself,
the only righteous judge, will place it on your head.

Presentation of Tithes and Offerings

The Lord has enriched the earth and crowned the year with bounty!
The hills and valleys, the pastures and meadows,
even the once barren wagon tracks
overflow with richness, plenty, and joy.
Shunning both greed and entitlement,
let us serve God's economy,
directing our gifts to those in genuine need.

Prayer of Dedication

O God,
who makes the earth abound, giving us every reason for gladness:
you have proven yourself trustworthy and faithful in all things.
Help us imitate your generous grace and your constant loyalty
by devoting our time and our energy,
our materials and our money,
to your work of building faithful disciples
and telling the world of your coming kingdom,
your abundant reign.
This we ask in Jesus' name.

The Charge and Blessing

Be ever ready for the Lord's appearing.
Indeed, may your hearts long to see it.
Be ever determined to fight the good fight.
Indeed, may your hopes arise with the Spirit.
Be ever prepared to empty yourselves in service.
For, indeed, your Creator will fill you again!

Proper 26
Ordinary Time 31 / October 30–November 5

Habakkuk 1:1–4; 2:1–4
Psalm 119:137–44
2 Thessalonians 1:1–4, 11–12
Luke 19:1–10

In Preparation for Worship

Almighty God,
give growth to the faith that is in me;
let your love increase within me;
fulfill by your power every good work,
every earnest resolution,
that the name of my Lord Jesus
may be glorified.

Call to Worship

The Lord is righteous and his judgments are right.
> **God's justice is everlasting and his law is truth.**

Be zealous for the Lord and do not forget the words of God.
> **Those who are small and those who are humble**
> **will not forget your precepts, O Lord.**

The promise of the Lord is tried and true.
> **Give us understanding that we may live**
> **in light of the promise of your approaching return!**

Opening Prayer

Come, Holy One, and make us holy.
Come, Worthy One, and make us worthy.
Teach us, ever-faithful God,
for we would learn from you to be steadfast.
Move us, ever-loving God,
that the love we have for you and for one another
would always increase.
You have called us, O triune God,
you have called us and we are here.
Reveal your vision and make it plain,
that we might receive you and live by faith.

Call to Confession

The proud do not have the right spirit in them,
and judgment comes forth perverted.
But the decrees of the Lord are altogether righteous,
the Lord himself is always faithful,
and the righteous will live by faith.
Therefore, trusting in the gracious mercy of God,
let us confess our sin to God,
asking pardon of our King
and seeking to be made worthy of his kingdom.

Prayer of Confession

**Righteous God,
we confess that we have allowed
the law to go slack and justice to be perverted.
We have allowed unclean and idolatrous things into our lives,
which cloud our vision, cause us to stumble,
and deprive you of the fidelity, obedience, and love you deserve from us.
We have sinned, fallen short, and offended your holiness.
Forgive us, O Lord!
Save us from the sins that we have committed
and spare us from their consequences.**

Keep us from temptation and affliction.
Protect your people from all that would threaten or harm us,
for by your grace, we still belong to you, in Jesus' name.

Declaration of Forgiveness

Christ Jesus our Lord came to seek and save the lost.
The Son of Man was rejected by many
because he ate and drank with sinners.
Yet his errand from heaven to earth to death and back
was precisely for the sake of sinners;
thus salvation has come to all who know themselves to be sinners
and who receive Christ in faith for who he is and for what he has done.
Know that you too are forgiven,
according to the grace of our God
and the Lord Jesus Christ.

Presentation of Tithes and Offerings

The salvation of God is evident in our lives
when we are freed from the fetters of worldly accumulation
and freely give with the generosity of those who know
their treasure is stored up in heaven.
Therefore, let us use our earthly wealth
in ways that demonstrate where our true citizenship lies,
under the lordship of the one
who has given us all things.

Prayer of Dedication

Receive, O God, these gifts, given humbly, given in faith.
For we cannot claim we deserve them or deserve to keep them.
But rather, as they have come to us from you,
we would have you bless them
and devote them to your fruitful work,
for the glory of your coming kingdom,
and in the name of our coming King,
Jesus Christ our Lord.

The Charge and Blessing

Go in the assurance of the presence of God,
ever anticipating his coming again,
ever longing for that day when we will marvel at Jesus
in all his power and his glory.
Prepare a place for him
in your hearts and in your homes,
that when he comes
you will be ready to receive him,
even as you hope to be received.

All Saints' Day
November 1 (or *First Sunday in November*)

Daniel 7:1–3, 15–18

Psalm 149

Ephesians 1:11–23

Luke 6:20–31

In Preparation for Worship

O God Most High,
Lord of all and the revealer of all truth:
though diverse worldly powers would trouble and unsettle us,
we fear you alone, you who are merciful,
you who have promised that your holy ones
shall receive the kingdom and possess it forever.
Open your realm to us at this time and place,
in defiance of every false power,
that we may worship you
in the splendor of your holiness.

Call to Worship

Praise the Lord! Sing to the Lord a new song,
his praise in the assembly of the faithful.
> **Let Israel be glad in its Maker;**
> **let the children of Zion rejoice in their King.**

Let them praise his name with dancing,
making melody to him with tambourine and lyre.
> **For the Lord takes pleasure in his people;**
> **he adorns the humble with victory.**

Let the faithful exult in glory;
let them sing for joy on their couches.
> **Let the high praises of God be in their throats**
> **and two-edged swords in their hands.**

This is glory for all his faithful ones.
> **Praise the Lord!**

OR

Come and remember the saints of God
in the presence of our Lord Jesus Christ.
> **Let us give thanks for their lives and for our fellowship with them.**
> **For the lives of the saints proclaim the reign of the Lord!**

Come and eat. Partake of God's word.
Come and receive the bread of true life.
> **Let us drink of the cup of the new covenant.**
> **Let us rejoice in God's promise of eternal life,**
> **for the Lamb of God has given his own blood to seal it.**

Opening Prayer

O Lord our God, giver of life and of eternal life,
you have displayed your power in raising Christ Jesus from the dead
and in seating him at your right hand in the heavenly places,
far above all rule and authority, all power and dominion,
and above every name.
We give you thanks for the unmerited gift of saving faith in our Lord Jesus
and for your love toward all the saints, and for this reason,
we look forward to eternity, wherein our praise and thanksgiving
will be ceaseless and unbroken;
for you, O God, have made Jesus the head over all things for the church;
his is the fullness that fills all in all.
Fill us, therefore, with your Holy Spirit,
that our worship on earth might well reflect
the worship you rightly enjoy in heaven,
amidst all of your holy saints and angels;
this we ask in Jesus' name.

All Saints' Day — November 1

Call to Confession

Although, in the end, God's holy people shall participate in the judgment of the nations, our calling for the present is to undergo sanctification, to examine our own deeds, to search our own hearts, to give an accounting for our sins, along with the sins of the church and the world; let us confess our sins against God and our neighbors, confident that God desires and has already arranged for our absolution.

Prayer of Confession

Righteous God, we confess we often shrink from what Jesus called blessed: poverty, hunger, weeping, and suffering for the name of Christ; in doing so, we risk losing sight of your kingdom with its immeasurable, but deferred, consolations and joys. Forgive us, O God, for seeking immediate pleasure, shunning sacrifice for others, and laboring for temporary, earthly rewards at the exclusion of eternal, heavenly treasure. Give us true, disciplined hearts, willing to weep now, to fast and pray for the lasting rewards of your coming kingdom; renew our sense of your priorities, that we may live by them, that we may serve you above all, serve others in genuine truth and love, and thereby live faithfully, in Jesus' name.

Declaration of Forgiveness [Ephesians 1:11-14]

Friends, hear and believe the good news! "In Christ we have obtained an inheritance, having been destined according to God's purpose who accomplishes all things according to his counsel and will, so that we, who have set our hope on Christ, might live for the praise of his glory. When you first heard the word of truth, the gospel of your salvation, and had believed in him, you were marked in Christ with the seal of the promised Holy Spirit; this is the pledge of our inheritance toward redemption as God's own people, to the praise of his glory." Know therefore that you are forgiven and be at peace.

Presentation of Tithes and Offerings

Jesus has commanded us to love even our enemies, to do good and bless even those who hate and curse his saints, and to pray for them. Therefore, since we are called to hold nothing back, let us give without expectation of return, assured that such giving is of the Lord and that our reward is simply in aspiring to do for others as Christ has done for us.

Prayer of Dedication [Ephesians 1:17–19]

O Father of glory and God of our Lord Jesus Christ,
grant us, we pray, your spirit of wisdom and revelation
as we grow in our knowledge of you, so that,
with the eyes of our hearts enlightened,
we may know the hope to which you have called us,
what are the riches of his glorious inheritance among the saints,
and what is the immeasurable greatness of his power for those who believe,
according to the working of his great power.
May your great power be at work in and through us
as we place these gifts at your feet
and use them for the praise of your glory,
in Jesus' name.

The Charge and Blessing

Go with the eyes of your heart enlightened,
in the knowledge of the hope to which God has called you.
Go in the immeasurable greatness of the Spirit's power
for those who believe in Jesus Christ.
Go in the love of the saints of God,
with strength to endure the loss of all things
for the sake of gaining the glory of heaven.

Proper 27
Ordinary Time 32 / November 6–12

Haggai 1:15b—2:9

Psalm 145:1–5, 17–21 OR Psalm 98

2 Thessalonians 2:1–5, 13–17

Luke 20:27–38

In Preparation for Worship

Living God,
let me never consort with the wicked,
but let me praise you in all things
and come fully to life!

Call to Worship

Great is the Lord and greatly to be praised.
God's greatness is unsearchable.
> **Every day I will bless you, my God and King.**
> **I will praise your name forever and ever.**

Come and declare God's greatness to the young.
Worship the Lord and meditate on God's works.
> **With my mouth I will praise the Lord at all times.**
> **Let all people praise the wonder of God.**

O sing to the Lord a new song.
Make a joyful noise to the Lord, all the earth.
> **For the ends of the earth have seen the victory of our God.**
> **Let all creation sing for joy.**

Opening Prayer

Lord Jesus, make us your people of the resurrection,
like angels in heaven, as children of God.
Open up heaven and eternity, we pray,
even as we worship you on earth
in anticipation of your coming, your final summing up.
Grant us the fullness of your Holy Spirit, O Christ.
We seek you with all our hearts.

Call to Confession

The Lord is coming soon to judge the earth.
The Lord will bring equity and true justice.
The wicked are destroyed,
while those who love God will be shown
tender mercy and steadfast love.
As trusting children approach
a kind and compassionate parent,
let us confess our sins to our loving God.

Prayer of Confession

**Merciful God,
each time we have departed from your teachings,
we have risked losing ourselves in chaos and ruin.
Cleverly searching for loopholes in your law,
we miss the great joys and the rich blessings
with which you reward your obedient children.
Forgive, preserve, and watch over us, O God.
Show us how to be your true and faithful church.
Remake us in Christ, to your exceeding glory.**

Declaration of Forgiveness

Do not be shaken.
Stand firm in your faith.
God has chosen you from the beginning
to receive salvation.
Through Christ you are made holy
by the Spirit of sanctification,

and in Christ you have reason to trust in the truth.
Know that you belong to God
and be at peace.

Presentation of Tithes and Offerings

All the riches of the earth
belong to the Lord of hosts:
all silver and gold,
the bounty of the sea
and the fruit of the dry land.
Though heaven and earth be shaken,
we have nothing to fear,
for God is with us.
The Lord has promised to prosper and restore us,
and multiply our former splendor.
Therefore, let us offer our earthly blessings,
that the Spirit of the Lord
might direct us in their use.

Prayer of Dedication

Almighty God,
there are few among us who remember
the former glory of this place.
We are but a remnant of your people,
seeking to be faithful in all things,
in our use of time and the treasure entrusted to us.
We can do nothing without your Spirit to guide us.
We can build nothing unless you provide vision and growth.
Let your light shine through our work,
your joy inspire our dreams,
your grace ignite our gratitude,
your love embrace this family of faith,
that all who witness our life together
may say to one another:
It is of the Lord!

The Blessing

Now may our Lord Jesus Christ himself and God our Father,
who loved us and through grace gave us eternal comfort and good hope,
comfort your hearts and strengthen them in every good work and word.

Proper 28
Ordinary Time 33 / November 13–19

Isaiah 65:17–25

Isaiah 12

2 Thessalonians 3:6–13

Luke 21:5–19

In Preparation for Worship

Draw us near, O Lord,
to your holy mountain;
reveal to us your new creation;
for we long for harmony with you,
with ourselves, with one another,
and with every creature in your kingdom of peace.

Call to Worship

Sing praises to the Lord, for he has done gloriously;
let it be known in all the earth.
> **Shout aloud and sing for joy, O royal Zion,**
> **for great in your midst is the Holy One of Israel.**

The Lord has spoken: "Be glad and rejoice forever in what I am creating;
for I am about to create Jerusalem as a joy, and its people as a delight.
> **"They shall not labor in vain, or bear children for calamity;**
> **for they shall be offspring blessed by the Lord—**
> **and their descendants as well."**

Let us worship God!

Opening Prayer

Eternal God, you are sovereign over all things,
over heaven and earth, over history and the eons,
and you call us to endure in faith until the end.
Come to us, we pray, and speak to us of the things that are coming,
those that should alert us and make us wary,
and those that are cause for joyful anticipation;
give us such faith that will not bow to fear,
and such fear that is reserved for you alone,
you who are both holy and gracious,
righteous and merciful.
This we ask in Jesus' name.

OR

Holy Lord, God of our salvation,
you are our strength and our might.
Grant that we may, in this hour, and at each moment of every day,
draw water from your wells of salvation
and drink deeply from your springs of living water.
Let your Spirit dwell among us and fill us beyond measure,
that we might forever be a people of praise, a joy and a delight to you,
and a true fellowship of Christian love for one another
and for all whom your Spirit would lead into our midst.
This we ask in Jesus' name. Amen.

Call to Confession

The Lord envisions a future for his people
that is joyful and peaceful, free of hurt and destruction, saying,
"I am about to create new heavens and a new earth;
the former things shall not be remembered or come to mind.
I will rejoice in Jerusalem, and delight in my people;
no more shall the sound of weeping be heard in it, or the cry of distress.
Before they call I will answer, while they are yet speaking I will hear."
Therefore, since it God's good pleasure
to confer on you his peaceable kingdom,
let us confess our sins, respectful of God's holy majesty and might,
yet confident of the Lord's gracious will.

OR

The Lord is about to create new heavens and a new earth.
The former things will no longer be remembered or come to mind.
No more will the sound of weeping be heard or the cry of distress.
No more will there be inequity or injustice.
But those who would have a share in this new creation
must renounce and surrender the former ways of sin and selfishness.

Prayer of Confession

Lord God, our hope of salvation,
we confess that we have been easily led astray from your ways;
when at labor, we quickly grow weary;
when at rest, we soon grow idle, proud, entitled, and privileged,
thinking little of burdening others.
Respecting the future, we permit fear and anxiety
to displace the trust and confidence we should rightly place in you.
Forgive us, O God, and remember not our sin;
grant us the mercy that you well know we need,
and restore us to good fellowship with you and with one another,
in Jesus' name.

OR

Saving God, we live in a world where not all have faith.
We confess that we too have often allowed ourselves
to lapse from faith into sin.
We have failed to exercise faith as we should,
to work for your ends,
to serve others under your guidance and authority,
and to lovingly build up faith in others.
Forgive us, Lord, for our frequent idleness in matters of faith
and in the lasting, redeeming, and fruitful work of your Spirit.
Redirect our hearts, O Lord, according to your love
and the faithfulness of Christ Jesus, in whose name we pray.

Declaration of Forgiveness

Give thanks to the Lord and praise his name,
who has turned away his anger and comforted his people.
Surely the Lord God is our salvation, our strength, and our might;
therefore, we will trust and not be afraid.
With joy let us draw water from the wells of salvation.
Let us make known God's saving deeds among the nations
and proclaim that his name is exalted,
for in the name of Jesus Christ, we are forgiven.

OR

Thus says the Lord:
Before they call I will answer, while they are yet speaking I will hear.
Trust in the Lord, and do not be afraid.
For the Lord has turned away his anger
and he offers you his Holy Spirit
for your refreshment, comfort, and consolation.
The Lord himself is not against us,
but he himself has become our salvation!
This is how you may know that you are truly forgiven and be at peace.

Presentation of Tithes and Offerings

God's new creation is one in which there shall no more be
infants who live but a few days,
or elders who do not live out a lifetime.
But those who build shall inhabit their own houses;
those who plant shall enjoy their fruit.
There shall be justice, freedom, and peace
under the gracious sovereignty of God.
With hopeful expectancy of Christ's coming kingdom,
let us render unto God our tithes and offerings.

Prayer of Dedication

From our labors, O God, we present these gifts,
that by your grace they might be of service to your new creation;
bless them, we pray, and give them increase;
show us how they may be best used in keeping with your sovereign will
and for your honor and glory; in Jesus' name.

The Charge and Blessing

Do not grow weary in doing what is right,
but do all your work well in the Lord,
giving others a good example to imitate;
fear neither the times, nor rumors, nor the portents of the age,
but stand fast on the promises of God
and hold fast to the prophecies of Scripture,
placing all your trust in our Lord Jesus Christ to fulfill his purposes,
for the glory of the triune God and for the joy of all the saints of heaven.

OR

The Lord strengthen and protect you.
The Lord direct your hearts to the love of God.
The Lord keep you in the faithfulness and the steadfastness of Christ Jesus,
himself the Lord of peace,
who will give you peace at all times and in every way.

Proper 29
Ordinary Time 34 / November 20–26
(*Christ the King* or *Reign of Christ*)

Jeremiah 23:1–6

Luke 1:68–79

Colossians 1:11–20

Luke 23:33–43

In Preparation for Worship

O Lord Jesus Christ,
you are our righteousness,
under whose reign we shall not fear,
for you rule wisely and execute justice for your people!
May you be first in our hearts and minds,
foremost in everything,
O Christ our King!

Call to Worship

Blessed be the Lord God of Israel,
who has looked with favor upon us and redeemed us!
>   **Our God has raised up a mighty savior!**

Blessed be the Lord God of Israel, who has given us
knowledge of our salvation by the forgiveness of our sins!
>   **Let us serve the Lord without fear,**
>   **in holiness, righteousness, and truth!**

By the tender mercy of our God, the dawn from on high will soon
break upon us, to give light to those who sit in darkness!

**We will trust and obey our Shepherd King,
the L****ORD**** Most High, to lead us in the way of peace!**

OPENING PRAYER

Sovereign Christ, you are the firstborn of all creation,
the perfect image of our invisible God!
In you all things in heaven and on earth,
both visible and invisible, were made.
You are the firstborn of the dead, and head of the church.
We praise you and thank you, O Christ our King!

OR

O Lord Jesus Christ, you are our righteousness,
under whose reign we will not fear,
for you rule wisely and execute justice for your people!
May you always be first in our hearts and minds,
foremost in everything, O Christ our King! Amen.

CALL TO CONFESSION

Any pleasure to be found in sin is false and fleeting.
But what eternal joy there is to be found
in recognizing all God has done to bring about our reconciliation!
For it is in the forgiveness of sins that we learn and know
the greatness of our salvation;
and, within this grace, the Spirit guides us in the ways of peace.
Therefore, let us bring into the light of God
those things we are otherwise inclined to consign to the shadows.

PRAYER OF CONFESSION

**Loving Lord, have mercy upon us.
Though you died to make peace
through your blood on the cross,
we have not been at peace.
Though you seek to strengthen us
by the gift of your glorious power,
we continue to rely on ourselves in our weakness.
Forgive us, O Lord, for each time**

we have failed to exalt or obey you as Ruler of our lives.
Reconcile us, O Christ,
to you and to one another, for your glory!

Declaration of Forgiveness

"The Lord is our righteousness." That is his name.
When his kingdom is established on earth,
he shall reign and deal wisely and execute justice in the land.
What is more, he will surely remember you,
whom he has rescued from the power of darkness
and transferred into his kingdom;
for in Christ, we have redemption, the forgiveness of our sins.
Thanks be to Jesus Christ our King!

Presentation of Tithes and Offerings

Christ is the head of the church;
he is the beginning, the firstborn from the dead,
so that he might come to have first place in everything.
For in Jesus Christ, all the fullness of God was pleased to dwell.
Therefore, let us offer our gifts accordingly, fearing no shortage,
but exalting Jesus Christ above all things,
that what we give may be placed at Christ's disposal
for the service to which he has called the church.

Prayer of Dedication

Our sovereign Lord, Jesus Christ,
refusing to save yourself, you came into your kingdom,
a company of redeemed sinners for whom you made peace
with God by the blood of your cross.
We can scarcely comprehend such a purchase,
such an inheritance, but we trust you,
with the heavenly Father and the Holy Spirit,
to administer your heritage and to reign over all things
as no one else can.
Bless therefore these gifts that they may serve
your royal and redemptive purposes,
and extol your glory.

THE CHARGE AND BLESSING

Go in the Lord to prepare his ways,
preaching salvation in Christ by the forgiveness of sins;
and may the light of our merciful God
break upon all who sit in darkness and in the shadow of death,
and guide your feet in the way of peace.

Index of Scripture Readings

TEXT	EVENT	PAGE
Genesis 11:1–9	Pentecost	135
Genesis 15:1–12, 17–18	Second Sunday in Lent	70
Genesis 45:3–11, 15	Seventh Sunday After Epiphany / Proper 2—Ordinary Time 7	51
Exodus 12:1–4 (5–10) 11–14	Maundy Thursday [ABC]	98
Exodus 34:29–35	Last Sunday After Epiphany *(Transfiguration Sunday)*	57
Deuteronomy 26:1–11	First Sunday in Lent	67
Joshua 5:9–12	Fourth Sunday in Lent	76
1 Samuel 2:18–20, 26	First Sunday After Christmas	24
1 Kings 17:8–16 (17–24)	Proper 5—Ordinary Time 10	148
1 Kings 18:20–21 (22–29) 30–39	Proper 4—Ordinary Time 9	144
1 Kings 19:1–4 (5–7) 8–15a	Proper 7—Ordinary Time 12	154
1 Kings 21:1–10 (11–14) 15–21a	Proper 6—Ordinary Time 11	151
2 Kings 2:1–2, 6–14	Proper 8—Ordinary Time 13	157

TEXT	EVENT	PAGE
2 Kings 5:1–14	Proper 9—Ordinary Time 14	160
Nehemiah 8:1–3, 5–6, 8–10	Third Sunday After Epiphany—Ordinary Time 3	39
Psalm 1	Sixth Sunday After Epiphany / Proper 1—Ordinary Time 6	48
Psalm 5:1–8	Proper 6—Ordinary Time 11	151
Psalm 8	Trinity Sunday	141
Psalm 14	Proper 19—Ordinary Time 24	192
Psalm 19	Third Sunday After Epiphany—Ordinary Time 3	39
Psalm 22	Good Friday [ABC]	101
Psalm 23	Fourth Sunday of Easter	119
Psalm 25:1–10	First Sunday of Advent	3
Psalm 27	Second Sunday in Lent	70
Psalm 29	First Sunday After Epiphany—Ordinary Time 1	33
Psalm 30	Third Sunday of Easter	115
Psalm 30	Proper 9—Ordinary Time 14	160
Psalm 31:9–16	Sixth Sunday in Lent *(Passion Sunday)*	85
Psalm 32	Fourth Sunday in Lent	76
Psalm 36:5–10	Second Sunday After Epiphany—Ordinary Time 2	36
Psalm 36:5–11	Monday of Holy Week [ABC]	89
Psalm 37:1–11, 39–40	Seventh Sunday After Epiphany / Proper 2—Ordinary Time 7	51
Psalm 42	Proper 7—Ordinary Time 12	154
Psalm 43	Proper 7—Ordinary Time 12	154
Psalm 47	Ascension of the Lord [ABC]	128
Psalm 50:1–8, 22–23	Proper 14—Ordinary Time 19	177
Psalm 51:1–17	Ash Wednesday [ABC]	63
Psalm 52	Proper 11—Ordinary Time 16	167

TEXT	EVENT	PAGE
Psalm 63:1–8	Third Sunday in Lent	73
Psalm 65	Proper 25—Ordinary Time 30	212
Psalm 66:1–12	Proper 23—Ordinary Time 28	206
Psalm 67	Sixth Sunday of Easter	125
Psalm 70	Wednesday of Holy Week [ABC]	95
Psalm 71:1–6	Fourth Sunday After Epiphany—Ordinary Time 4	42
Psalm 71:1–6	Proper 16—Ordinary Time 21	183
Psalm 71:1–14	Tuesday of Holy Week [ABC]	92
Psalm 72:1–7, 10–14	Epiphany [ABC]	30
Psalm 77:1–2, 11–20	Proper 8—Ordinary Time 13	157
Psalm 79:1–9	Proper 20—Ordinary Time 25	195
Psalm 80:1–7	Fourth Sunday of Advent	12
Psalm 80:1–2, 8–19	Proper 15—Ordinary Time 20	180
Psalm 81:1, 10–16	Proper 17—Ordinary Time 22	186
Psalm 82	Proper 10—Ordinary Time 15	164
Psalm 85	Proper 12—Ordinary Time 17	170
Psalm 91:1–2, 9–16	First Sunday in Lent	67
Psalm 91:1–6, 14–16	Proper 21—Ordinary Time 26	199
Psalm 92:1–4, 12–15	Eighth Sunday After Epiphany / Proper 3—Ordinary Time 8	54
Psalm 93	Ascension of the Lord [ABC]	128
Psalm 96	Christmas, First Proper [ABC] (*Christmas Eve*)	15
Psalm 96	Proper 4—Ordinary Time 9	144
Psalm 97	Christmas, Second Proper [ABC] (*Christmas Morning*)	18
Psalm 97	Seventh Sunday of Easter	131
Psalm 98	Christmas, Third Proper [ABC] (*Christmas Day*)	21
Psalm 98	Proper 27—Ordinary Time 32	223
Psalm 99	Last Sunday After Epiphany (*Transfiguration Sunday*)	57

TEXT	EVENT	PAGE
Psalm 104:24–34, 35b	Pentecost	135
Psalm 107:1–9, 43	Proper 13—Ordinary Time 18	173
Psalm 114	Easter Evening [ABC]	109
Psalm 116:1–2, 12–19	Maundy Thursday [ABC]	98
Psalm 118:1–2, 19–29	Sixth Sunday in Lent *(Palm Sunday)*	82
Psalm 118:1–2, 14–24	Easter *(The Resurrection of the Lord)*	105
Psalm 118:14–29	Second Sunday of Easter	112
Psalm 119:97–104	Proper 24—Ordinary Time 29	209
Psalm 119:137–44	Proper 26—Ordinary Time 31	215
Psalm 126	Fifth Sunday in Lent	79
Psalm 137	Proper 22—Ordinary Time 27	203
Psalm 138	Fifth Sunday After Epiphany — Ordinary Time 5	45
Psalm 139:1–6, 13–18	Proper 18—Ordinary Time 23	189
Psalm 145:1–5, 17–21	Proper 27—Ordinary Time 32	223
Psalm 146	Proper 5—Ordinary Time 10	148
Psalm 147:12–20	Second Sunday After Christmas [ABC]	27
Psalm 148	First Sunday After Christmas	24
Psalm 148	Fifth Sunday of Easter	122
Psalm 149	All Saints' Day / November 1	219
Psalm 150	Second Sunday of Easter	112
Proverbs 8:1–4, 22–31	Trinity Sunday	141
Isaiah 1:1, 10–20	Proper 14—Ordinary Time 19	177
Isaiah 5:1–7	Proper 15—Ordinary Time 20	180
Isaiah 6:1–8 (9–13)	Fifth Sunday After Epiphany — Ordinary Time 5	45
Isaiah 9:2–7	Christmas, First Proper [ABC] *(Christmas Eve)*	15
Isaiah 12	Proper 28—Ordinary Time 33	227
Isaiah 12:2–6	Third Sunday of Advent	9

Index of Scripture Readings 241

TEXT	EVENT	PAGE
Isaiah 25:6–9	Easter Evening [ABC]	109
Isaiah 42:1–9	Monday of Holy Week [ABC]	89
Isaiah 43:1–7	First Sunday After Epiphany—Ordinary Time 1	33
Isaiah 43:16–21	Fifth Sunday in Lent	79
Isaiah 49:1–7	Tuesday of Holy Week [ABC]	92
Isaiah 50:4–9a	Sixth Sunday in Lent *(Palm Sunday)*	82
Isaiah 50:4–9a	Sixth Sunday in Lent *(Passion Sunday)*	85
Isaiah 50:4–9a	Wednesday of Holy Week [ABC]	95
Isaiah 52:7–10	Christmas, Third Proper [ABC] *(Christmas Day)*	21
Isaiah 52:12—53:12	Good Friday [ABC]	101
Isaiah 55:1–9	Third Sunday in Lent	73
Isaiah 55:10–13	Eighth Sunday After Epiphany / Proper 3—Ordinary Time 8	54
Isaiah 58:1–12	Ash Wednesday [ABC]	63
Isaiah 60:1–6	Epiphany [ABC]	30
Isaiah 62:1–5	Second Sunday After Epiphany—Ordinary Time 2	36
Isaiah 62:6–12	Christmas, Second Proper [ABC] *(Christmas Morning)*	18
Isaiah 65:17–25	Easter *(The Resurrection of the Lord)*	105
Isaiah 65:17–25	Proper 28—Ordinary Time 33	227
Jeremiah 1:4–10	Fourth Sunday After Epiphany—Ordinary Time 4	42
Jeremiah 1:4–10	Proper 16—Ordinary Time 21	183
Jeremiah 2:4–13	Proper 17—Ordinary Time 22	186
Jeremiah 4:11–12, 22–28	Proper 19—Ordinary Time 24	192
Jeremiah 8:18—9:1	Proper 20—Ordinary Time 25	195
Jeremiah 17:5–10	Sixth Sunday After Epiphany / Proper 1—Ordinary Time 6	48
Jeremiah 18:1–11	Proper 18—Ordinary Time 23	189

TEXT	EVENT	PAGE
Jeremiah 23:1–6	Proper 29—Ordinary Time 34 (*Christ the King* or *Reign of Christ*)	232
Jeremiah 29:1, 4–7	Proper 23—Ordinary Time 28	206
Jeremiah 31:7–14	Second Sunday After Christmas [ABC]	27
Jeremiah 31:27–34	Proper 24—Ordinary Time 29	209
Jeremiah 32:1–3a, 6–15	Proper 21—Ordinary Time 26	199
Jeremiah 33:14–16	First Sunday of Advent	3
Lamentations 1:1–6	Proper 22—Ordinary Time 27	203
Lamentations 3:19–26	Proper 22—Ordinary Time 27	203
Daniel 7:1–3, 15–18	All Saints' Day / November 1	219
Hosea 1:2–10	Proper 12—Ordinary Time 17	170
Hosea 11:1–11	Proper 13—Ordinary Time 18	173
Joel 2:1–2, 12–17	Ash Wednesday [ABC]	63
Joel 2:23–32	Proper 25—Ordinary Time 30	212
Amos 7:7–17	Proper 10—Ordinary Time 15	164
Amos 8:1–12	Proper 11—Ordinary Time 16	167
Micah 5:2–5a	Fourth Sunday of Advent	12
Habakkuk 1:1–4; 2:1–4	Proper 26—Ordinary Time 31	215
Zephaniah 3:14–20	Third Sunday of Advent	9
Haggai 1:15b—2:9	Proper 27—Ordinary Time 32	223
Malachi 3:1–4	Second Sunday of Advent	6

Index of Scripture Readings

TEXT	EVENT	PAGE
Matthew 2:1–12	Epiphany [ABC]	30
Matthew 6:1–6, 16–21	Ash Wednesday [ABC]	63
Luke 3:7–18	Third Sunday of Advent	9
Luke 1:39–40 (46–55)	Fourth Sunday of Advent	12
Luke 1:47–55	Fourth Sunday of Advent	12
Luke 1:68–79	Second Sunday of Advent	6
Luke 1:68–79	Proper 29—Ordinary Time 34 (*Christ the King* or *Reign of Christ*)	232
Luke 2:1–14 (15–20)	Christmas, First Proper [ABC] (*Christmas Eve*)	15
Luke 2:(1–7) 8–20	Christmas, Second Proper [ABC] (*Christmas Morning*)	18
Luke 2:41–52	First Sunday After Christmas	24
Luke 3:1–6	Second Sunday of Advent	6
Luke 3:15–17, 21–22	First Sunday After Epiphany—Ordinary Time 1	33
Luke 4:1–13	First Sunday in Lent	67
Luke 4:14–21	Third Sunday After Epiphany—Ordinary Time 3	39
Luke 4:21–30	Fourth Sunday After Epiphany—Ordinary Time 4	42
Luke 5:1–11	Fifth Sunday After Epiphany — Ordinary Time 5	45
Luke 6:17–26	Sixth Sunday After Epiphany / Proper 1—Ordinary Time 6	48
Luke 6:20–31	All Saints' Day / November 1	219
Luke 6:27–38	Seventh Sunday After Epiphany / Proper 2—Ordinary Time 7	51
Luke 6:39–49	Eighth Sunday After Epiphany / Proper 3—Ordinary Time 8	54
Luke 7:1–10	Proper 4—Ordinary Time 9	144
Luke 7:11–17	Proper 5—Ordinary Time 10	148
Luke 7:36—8:3	Proper 6—Ordinary Time 11	151
Luke 8:26–39	Proper 7—Ordinary Time 12	154

Index of Scripture Readings

TEXT	EVENT	PAGE
Luke 9:28–36 (37–43)	Last Sunday After Epiphany *(Transfiguration Sunday)*	57
Luke 9:51–62	Proper 8—Ordinary Time 13	157
Luke 10:1–11, 16–20	Proper 9—Ordinary Time 14	160
Luke 10:25–37	Proper 10—Ordinary Time 15	164
Luke 10:38–42	Proper 11—Ordinary Time 16	167
Luke 11:1–13	Proper 12—Ordinary Time 17	170
Luke 12:13–21	Proper 13—Ordinary Time 18	173
Luke 12:32–40	Proper 14—Ordinary Time 19	177
Luke 12:49–56	Proper 15—Ordinary Time 20	180
Luke 13:1–9	Third Sunday in Lent	73
Luke 13:10–17	Proper 16—Ordinary Time 21	183
Luke 13:31–35	Second Sunday in Lent	70
Luke 14:1, 7–14	Proper 17—Ordinary Time 22	186
Luke 14:25–33	Proper 18—Ordinary Time 23	189
Luke 15:1–10	Proper 19—Ordinary Time 24	192
Luke 15:1–3, 11b–32	Fourth Sunday in Lent	76
Luke 16:1–13	Proper 20—Ordinary Time 25	195
Luke 16:19–31	Proper 21—Ordinary Time 26	199
Luke 17:5–10	Proper 22—Ordinary Time 27	203
Luke 17:11–19	Proper 23—Ordinary Time 28	206
Luke 18:1–8	Proper 24—Ordinary Time 29	209
Luke 18:9–14	Proper 25—Ordinary Time 30	212
Luke 19:1–10	Proper 26—Ordinary Time 31	215
Luke 19:28–40	Sixth Sunday in Lent *(Palm Sunday)*	82
Luke 20:27–38	Proper 27—Ordinary Time 32	223
Luke 21:5–19	Proper 28—Ordinary Time 33	227
Luke 21:25–36	First Sunday of Advent	3
Luke 22:14–23:56	Sixth Sunday in Lent *(Passion Sunday)*	85
Luke 23:1–49	Sixth Sunday in Lent *(Passion Sunday)*	85
Luke 23:33–43	Proper 29—Ordinary Time 34 *(Christ the King* or *Reign of Christ)*	232

Index of Scripture Readings   245

TEXT	EVENT	PAGE
Luke 24:1–12	Easter *(The Resurrection of the Lord)*	105
Luke 24:13–49	Easter Evening [ABC]	109
Luke 24:44–53	Ascension of the Lord [ABC]	128
John 1:1–14	Christmas, Third Proper [ABC] *(Christmas Day)*	21
John 1:(1–9) 10–18	Second Sunday After Christmas [ABC]	27
John 2:1–11	Second Sunday After Epiphany—Ordinary Time 2	36
John 5:1–9	Sixth Sunday of Easter	125
John 10:22–30	Fourth Sunday of Easter	119
John 12:1–8	Fifth Sunday in Lent	79
John 12:1–11	Monday of Holy Week [ABC]	89
John 12:20–36	Tuesday of Holy Week [ABC]	92
John 13:1–17, 31b–35	Maundy Thursday [ABC]	98
John 13:21–32	Wednesday of Holy Week [ABC]	95
John 13:31–35	Fifth Sunday of Easter	122
John 14:8–17 (25–27)	Pentecost	135
John 14:23–29	Sixth Sunday of Easter	125
John 16:12–15	Trinity Sunday	141
John 17:20–26	Seventh Sunday of Easter	131
John 18:1—19:42	Good Friday [ABC]	101
John 20:1–18	Easter *(The Resurrection of the Lord)*	105
John 20:19–31	Second Sunday of Easter	112
John 21:1–19	Third Sunday of Easter	115
Acts 1:1–11	Ascension of the Lord [ABC]	128
Acts 2:1–21	Pentecost	135
Acts 5:27–32	Second Sunday of Easter	112
Acts 8:14–17	First Sunday After Epiphany—Ordinary Time 1	33
Acts 9:1–6 (7–20)	Third Sunday of Easter	115

Index of Scripture Readings

TEXT	EVENT	PAGE
Acts 9:36–43	Fourth Sunday of Easter	119
Acts 10:34–43	Easter *(The Resurrection of the Lord)*	105
Acts 11:1–18	Fifth Sunday of Easter	122
Acts 16:9–15	Sixth Sunday of Easter	125
Acts 16:16–34	Seventh Sunday of Easter	131
Romans 5:1–5	Trinity Sunday	141
Romans 8:14–17	Pentecost	135
Romans 10:8b–13	First Sunday in Lent	67
1 Corinthians 1:18–31	Tuesday of Holy Week [ABC]	92
1 Corinthians 5:6b–8	Easter Evening [ABC]	109
1 Corinthians 10:1–13	Third Sunday in Lent	73
1 Corinthians 11:23–26	Maundy Thursday [ABC]	98
1 Corinthians 12:1–11	Second Sunday After Epiphany—Ordinary Time 2	36
1 Corinthians 12:12–31a	Third Sunday After Epiphany—Ordinary Time 3	39
1 Corinthians 13:1–13	Fourth Sunday After Epiphany—Ordinary Time 4	42
1 Corinthians 15:1–11	Fifth Sunday After Epiphany — Ordinary Time 5	45
1 Corinthians 15:12–20	Sixth Sunday After Epiphany / Proper 1—Ordinary Time 6	48
1 Corinthians 15:19–26	Easter *(The Resurrection of the Lord)*	105
1 Corinthians 15:35–38, 42–50	Seventh Sunday After Epiphany / Proper 2—Ordinary Time 7	51
1 Corinthians 15:51–58	Eighth Sunday After Epiphany / Proper 3—Ordinary Time 8	54
2 Corinthians 3:12–4:2	Last Sunday After Epiphany *(Transfiguration Sunday)*	57
2 Corinthians 5:16–21	Fourth Sunday in Lent	76
2 Corinthians 5:20b–6:10	Ash Wednesday [ABC]	63

Index of Scripture Readings 247

TEXT	EVENT	PAGE
Galatians 1:1–12	Proper 4—Ordinary Time 9	144
Galatians 1:11–24	Proper 5—Ordinary Time 10	148
Galatians 2:15–21	Proper 6—Ordinary Time 11	151
Galatians 3:23–29	Proper 7—Ordinary Time 12	154
Galatians 5:1, 13–25	Proper 8—Ordinary Time 13	157
Galatians 6:(1–6) 7–16	Proper 9—Ordinary Time 14	160
Ephesians 1:3–14	Second Sunday After Christmas [ABC]	27
Ephesians 1:11–23	All Saints' Day / November 1	219
Ephesians 1:15–23	Ascension of the Lord [ABC]	128
Ephesians 3:1–12	Epiphany [ABC]	30
Philippians 1:3–11	Second Sunday of Advent	6
Philippians 2:5–11	Sixth Sunday in Lent *(Palm Sunday)*	82
Philippians 2:5–11	Sixth Sunday in Lent *(Passion Sunday)*	85
Philippians 3:4b–14	Fifth Sunday in Lent	79
Philippians 3:17—4:1	Second Sunday in Lent	70
Philippians 4:4–7	Third Sunday of Advent	9
Colossians 1:1–14	Proper 10—Ordinary Time 15	164
Colossians 1:11–20	Proper 29—Ordinary Time 34 *(Christ the King* or *Reign of Christ)*	232
Colossians 1:15–28	Proper 11—Ordinary Time 16	167
Colossians 2:6–15 (16–19)	Proper 12—Ordinary Time 17	170
Colossians 3:1–11	Proper 13—Ordinary Time 18	173
Colossians 3:12–17	First Sunday After Christmas	24
1 Thessalonians 3:9–13	First Sunday of Advent	3
2 Thessalonians 1:1–4, 11–12	Proper 26—Ordinary Time 31	215
2 Thessalonians 2:1–5, 13–17	Proper 27—Ordinary Time 32	223

Index of Scripture Readings

TEXT	EVENT	PAGE
2 Thessalonians 3:6–13	Proper 28—Ordinary Time 33	227
1 Timothy 1:12–17	Proper 19—Ordinary Time 24	192
1 Timothy 2:1–7	Proper 20—Ordinary Time 25	195
1 Timothy 6:6–19	Proper 21—Ordinary Time 26	199
2 Timothy 1:1–14	Proper 22—Ordinary Time 27	203
2 Timothy 2:8–15	Proper 23—Ordinary Time 28	206
2 Timothy 3:14—4:5	Proper 24—Ordinary Time 29	209
2 Timothy 4:6–8, 16–18	Proper 25—Ordinary Time 30	212
Titus 2:11–14	Christmas, First Proper [ABC] (Christmas Eve)	15
Titus 3:4–7	Christmas, Second Proper [ABC] (Christmas Morning)	18
Philemon 1–21	Proper 18—Ordinary Time 23	189
Hebrews 1:1–4 (5–12)	Christmas, Third Proper [ABC] (Christmas Day)	21
Hebrews 4:14–16; 5:7–9	Good Friday [ABC]	101
Hebrews 9:11–15	Monday of Holy Week [ABC]	89
Hebrews 10:5–10	Fourth Sunday of Advent	12
Hebrews 10:16–25	Good Friday [ABC]	101
Hebrews 11:1–3, 8–16	Proper 14—Ordinary Time 19	177
Hebrews 11:29—12:2	Proper 15—Ordinary Time 20	180
Hebrews 12:1–3	Wednesday of Holy Week [ABC]	95
Hebrews 12:18–29	Proper 16—Ordinary Time 21	183
Hebrews 13:1–8, 15–16	Proper 17—Ordinary Time 22	186
Revelation 1:4–8	Second Sunday of Easter	112
Revelation 5:11–14	Third Sunday of Easter	115

TEXT	EVENT	PAGE
Revelation 7:9–17	Fourth Sunday of Easter	119
Revelation 21:1–6	Fifth Sunday of Easter	122
Revelation 21:10; 21:22—22:5	Sixth Sunday of Easter	125
Revelation 22:12–14, 16–17, 20–21	Seventh Sunday of Easter	131

www.ingramcontent.com/pod-product-compliance
Lightning Source LLC
Chambersburg PA
CBHW031725230426
43669CB00007B/244